The Big Quiz Book for Couples

MORE THAN 1100 QUESTIONS TO IMPROVE COMMUNICATION WITH YOUR PARTNER, BUILD A SOLID AND HEALTHY RELATIONSHIP, AND HAVE FUN TOGETHER!

Felicity L. Roberts

Table of Contents

Introduction

Think about it for a moment: why are you in a relationship? Did you hope to find someone who might complete you? A reflection of yourself, maybe?

Or did you just fall head over heels in love with your partner?

Probably that's what happened. In fact, this is what happens most of the time. We meet someone, and somehow we feel irresistibly attracted to this perfect human being who can basically do no wrong and will make us happy for the rest of our lives.

In short, we don't tend to think about "why" we want to be with this person in particular; we just follow our heart. And that's great (after all, there's no better feeling in the world than falling in love!), but making a relationship last requires a little more work. Primarily because, besides love and attraction, all human beings also need emotional intimacy, respect, and a sense of security.

And the first step to achieving all of this is to get to know your partner: who they are at their core, what they need, how they react in specific situations, the experiences that have shaped their life, what they want from their better half, and what they dream about their future.

And speaking of the future, not too long ago, we expected a romantic relationship to inevitably lead to marriage. Nowadays, not everyone shares this same vision, while many other people have a very different idea of marriage compared to what it was some decades ago. Instead of reflecting gender-based, specific roles, most marriages today are based on equal task division, sexual attraction, companionship, and mutual support.

No matter what kind of relationship you see in your future, if you want to make it work, sharing a similar vision with your partner and knowing what makes each other happy will surely help.

And this is precisely this book's goal: understanding your other half and their needs better and avoiding all those relationship mistakes resulting from a lack of communication.

In the following pages, you'll find more than 1100 questions that will help you, in a fun and exciting way, to get to know your sentimental companion and build a solid relationship with them. We'll start with "easier" questions about personality and things you like, and we'll then continue with more personal questions about your views on more serious topics and your hopes for the future of your relationship.

You can change this order according to your personal preferences and where you are in your relationship. Piece of advice? Remember that the best relationships are built on solid friendships, so it's wise first to address the questions that will help you build that kind of base.

Also, if you're at the very beginning of your love story, you might want to wait, at least a little bit, to ask questions about marriage and children... it could be better not to rush things, don't you think?

At the same time, try not to skip those questions that make you feel a little shy or embarrassed. Why? Because breaking down communication barriers and being able to talk about everything with your partner is a great way to build mutual trust.

Also, avoid answering the questions with what you think might please the other person instead of the truth: there's no point in being in a relationship if you can't be yourself around your partner!

Keep in mind that some questions have not been included for a very good reason. It's important to talk about what you like and don't like sexually or in a relationship, but sharing too many specific details of your past is definitely unnecessary. So, be honest in your answers; just try to avoid giving too much "graphic information" to your partner, or you might end up hurting their feelings.

As it's normal, you'll also find questions that don't apply to your relationship right now. If, for example, you and your partner are both in your sixties, you might probably want to skip the questions about how many children you would like to have.

However, while this book is more oriented towards couples in the initial stage of their journey together, long-time partners will still find hundreds of questions that need answering. And you can also choose to use the book the other way around! Imagine you and your partner have been together for 15 years: you can answer each other's questions to see how well you know one another after this time together.

Also, consider that your answers to several questions might change over time. What you feel righ now about, for example, moving to a small town in the countryside might be different in the future. So keep in mind that it can be fun to use this book again in a few years or to compare the answers you gave at one point in life with what you think now: you will have a good time and see how much you and your partner have evolved and grown together!

And how should you use this book in practice? It's entirely up to you and your partner. You may choose to answer five or six questions in a row or spend several hours answering as many questions as possible in a sitting. Suppose you've bought the paperback or hardcover version of this book. In that case, you can write your answers down (or at least the main points) on these same pages.
If you have bought the kindle version, or simply if you prefer so, you may answer the questions by email and send them to one another on the same day so that you will not influence each other in any way. And, of course, you can read each question out loud and answer them together, using this opportunity to talk and get to know each other better.

Once again, this book has only one "rule": always try to be honest and answer the truth. You and your partner must love each other for who you truly are and feel free to be yourselves around one another to build a solid and lasting relationship.

Have a great time together!

Who are you?

😀   PARTNER 1

🙂   PARTNER 2

Section 1: Understanding Your Personality

You'll find many different questions in this section. Why is that? Because your personality is at the core of who you are as a person and can really help your partner understand you better (and vice versa, of course!). Over the course of your life, you may change your mind about many things, but the experiences that have shaped your character and how you act and react in different situations will most likely always be a part of you.

So, are you ready?

1. Do you consider yourself an optimist, a pessimist, or somewhere in between?

☻ ....

☺ ....

2. Would you describe yourself as a troublemaker or a peacekeeper?

☻ ....

☺ ....

3. Are you a morning person, a night person, or somewhere in the middle?

☻ ....

☺ ....

4. *Are you generally in a good or a bad mood in the morning?*

☻ ....

☺ ....

5. *Do you consider yourself an emphatic person?*

☻ ....

☺ ....

6. *Do you tend to put the needs of others before your own?*

☻ ....

☺ ....

7. *Do you consider you have high or low self-esteem?*

☻ ....

☺ ....

8. *When you look at yourself in the mirror, what is the first thing that comes to your mind?*

☻ ....

☺ ....

9. *Have you ever felt inferior to someone?*

☻ ....

☺ ....

10. *Do you consider yourself a leader or a follower?*

☻ _____

☺ _____

11. *Do you need to always be in control, or can you delegate?*

☻ _____

☺ _____

12. *Do you consider yourself a dreamer or a pragmatic person?*

☻ _____

☺ _____

13. *How do you usually react when you receive a compliment?*

☻ _____

☺ _____

14. *How do you typically react when someone criticizes you?*

☻ _____

☺ _____

15. *How do you tend to react when you get upset?*

☻ _____

☺ _____

16. *Is there a particular trait in a person's character that irritates you?*

😃 --

🙂 --

17. *Is it easy for you to forgive and forget?*

😃 --

🙂 --

18. *Do you easily lose your temper?*

😃 --

🙂 --

19. *Have you ever been in a physical fight with someone? Why did it start?*

😃 --

🙂 --

20. *Do you think it can be appropriate to express anger in a physical way? If so, when and how?*

😃 --

🙂 --

21. *Is it difficult for you to compromise on things?*

😃 --

🙂 --

22. *Do you tend to overthink?*

☻ ---

☺ ---

23. *Do you tend to stress about things that you can't control?*

☻ ---

☺ ---

24. *Do you tend to be punctual, or are you usually late?*

☻ ---

☺ ---

25. *Do you feel like you waste a lot of time? Does that bother you?*

☻ ---

☺ ---

26. *Which is the number one thing that you consider a waste of time?*

☻ ---

☺ ---

27. *Do you enjoy being the center of attention?*

☻ ---

☺ ---

28. Would you consider yourself a generous person?

☻ --

☺ --

29. Are there any things you're selfish about?

☻ --

☺ --

30. Do you consider yourself able to react calmly in an emergency? Have you ever had to face a circumstance of this kind?

☻ --

☺ --

31. How do you manage yourself under stress?

☻ --

☺ --

32. Have you ever lost someone close to you? How did you handle this loss?

☻ --

☺ --

33. Have you ever lost a beloved pet? How did you feel?

☻ --

☺ --

34. *How do you generally handle trauma? It can be of any type, for example, a big disappointment, someone's passing, being fired, etc.*

😀 _____

☺ _____

35. *Do you cry often? What kind of circumstances bring you to tears?*

😀 _____

☺ _____

36. *Do you usually cry watching movies or TV shows?*

😀 _____

☺ _____

37. *What's your biggest fear?*

😀 _____

☺ _____

38. *Do your fears prevent you from doing the things you want, or are you able to manage them?*

😀 _____

☺ _____

39. *Are you camera shy? If yes, why?*

😀 _____

☺ _____

40. *Do you generally listen to your gut feeling? Is it mostly right or wrong?*

☻ ....

☺ ....

41. *Is there anything you have practically no self-control over (chocolate, fries, sales, new shoes, cars, etc.)?*

☻ ....

☺ ....

42. *What kind of feeling do you find controlling the most difficult?*

☻ ....

☺ ....

43. *What kind of feeling do you find expressing the most difficult?*

☻ ....

☺ ....

44. *Do you consider yourself an expert on a particular topic? Which one?*

☻ ....

☺ ....

45. *Do you consider yourself an organized person?*

☻ ....

☺ ....

46. *Do you usually make to-do lists?*

47. *Do you consider yourself a handy person?*

48. *Are there any rituals that you carry out every day?*

49. *How could someone determine whether you are happy or not? And if you're sad?*

50. *Do you consider yourself a sensible person?*

51. *Is there anything you worry about all the time?*

52. *Do you feel you're happier in a particular season? If so, why?*

☺ ....

☺ ....

53. *When did you feel the happiest in your life?*

☺ ....

☺ ....

54. *If you could live one year of your life all over again without changing a thing, what year would you choose? Why?*

☺ ....

☺ ....

55. *Do you think luck has played a huge role in your life so far?*

☺ ....

☺ ....

56. *Can you think of a specific moment when you turned your life around?*

☺ ....

☺ ....

57. *What are the three things that you have done in your life that you are most proud of?*

☺ ....

☺ ....

58. *And what are the three things you regret the most?*

☻ ---

☺ ---

59. *What was your greatest disappointment in life?*

☻ ---

☺ ---

60. *Have you ever worked really hard to achieve something, but it didn't pay off in the end?*

☻ ---

☺ ---

61. *In what ways do you feel blessed in your life?*

☻ ---

☺ ---

62. *Do you tend to stress a lot about everyday responsibilities?*

☻ ---

☺ ---

63. *What helps you to calm down and relax when you feel stressed out?*

☻ ---

☺ ---

64. How do you think you could enjoy life more?

☺ ---

☺ ---

65. What makes you feel important and valued the most in your life?

☺ ---

☺ ---

66. What makes life worth living, in your opinion?

☺ ---

☺ ---

67. When you feel sick, do you prefer to be alone or have someone staying close to you?

☺ ---

☺ ---

68. What do you think is the most caring and loving thing you have ever done for someone?

☺ ---

☺ ---

69. Would you prefer to live a calm and consistent (maybe a bit boring) life or one full of excitement and rocky patches?

☺ ---

☺ ---

70. *Do you consider your current life boring or interesting?*

☻ ---

☺ ---

71. *Do you like changes or prefer stability?*

☻ ---

☺ ---

72. *Can you adapt to change easily? Any example in this sense?*

☻ ---

☺ ---

73. *When you succeed in your goals, do you tend to be humble or boast about it?*

☻ ---

☺ ---

74. *Do you generally analyze your decisions before talking about them or the opposite?*

☻ ---

☺ ---

75. *Do you consider you tend to exaggerate things when talking to others? Why do you think you do that?*

☻ ---

☺ ---

76. Do you think you have a "childish" side? What parts of your life are affected in this sense?

☺ _____

☺ _____

77. What kind of social gathering do you prefer: a big party or a small group of close friends?

☺ _____

☺ _____

78. Would you describe yourself as the "life of the party"?

☺ _____

☺ _____

79. Are you more of an extrovert or an introvert? Or can this definition change depending on the people/situation around you?

☺ _____

☺ _____

80. Are you more of a people person or a solitary person?

☺ _____

☺ _____

81. Do you tend to keep your feelings to yourself, or do you prefer to share them openly?

☺ _____

☺ _____

82. *Do you tend to ask for help, or do you prefer to do everything on your own?*

😎 _____

🙂 _____

83. *Do you feel like you need to be emotionally supported by someone else in a time of problems? Or you rather face them by yourself?*

😎 _____

🙂 _____

84. *Do you trust people? Or is it something difficult for you?*

😎 _____

🙂 _____

85. *Do you like to speak in public? Or is it something that scares you?*

😎 _____

🙂 _____

86. *Do you like to be alone? Or do you need to be with people all the time?*

😎 _____

🙂 _____

87. *Have you ever lived alone? Do you or did you enjoy it?*

😎 _____

🙂 _____

88. *Have you ever lived with friends or other people? Did you enjoy it?*

☻ _____

☺ _____

89. *Do you know most of your neighbors? Do you socialize with them often?*

☻ _____

☺ _____

90. *Do you believe you are mature and experienced enough to maintain a successful long-term relationship?*

☻ _____

☺ _____

91. *Do you consider yourself as worthy of love? Why or why not?*

☻ _____

☺ _____

92. *Which do you think should have the final say in decisions: heart or mind? Why?*

☻ _____

☺ _____

93. *Which traits of your personality do you share with your family?*

☻ _____

☺ _____

94. *And in what way are you completely different from them?*

☺ ---

☺ ---

95. *Which personality traits do you admire in your parents and also look for in a partner?*

☺ ---

☺ ---

96. *Which is the thing that makes you feel homesick the most?*

☺ ---

☺ ---

97. *Do you consider yourself a jealous person?*

☺ ---

☺ ---

98. *Do you consider yourself a hugger?*

☺ ---

☺ ---

99. *Are you scared of being alone?*

☺ ---

☺ ---

100. What is the best thing about you when you're in a relationship?

☻ ....

☺ ....

101. And what is the worst?

☻ ....

☺ ....

102. Do you like giving or receiving gifts the most?

☻ ....

☺ ....

103. Which is the best gift you've ever received in your life? Why?

☻ ....

☺ ....

104. Are you good at remembering important dates, such as the anniversaries of the people you love?

☻ ....

☺ ....

105. Do you have good memories of your school years? If not, why?

☻ ....

☺ ....

106. *Is it easy for you to make new friends?*

😀 _____

🙂 _____

107. *Do you consider yourself more or less mature than your friends? Why?*

😀 _____

🙂 _____

108. *Do you consider any of your coworkers like real friends?*

😀 _____

🙂 _____

109. *Have you ever felt envious of a colleague? Why?*

😀 _____

🙂 _____

110. *In general, do you think you're good at keeping secrets? Or is it hard for you?*

😀 _____

🙂 _____

111. *Could you forgive a betrayal from a friend or partner? Have you before?*

😀 _____

🙂 _____

112. *Do you think you are a competitive person? Especially in what areas?*

😀 _____

🙂 _____

113. *Do you enjoy debating?*

😀 _____

🙂 _____

114. *How do you feel when someone close to you disagrees with you?*

😀 _____

🙂 _____

115. *Do you always need to have the last word?*

😀 _____

🙂 _____

116. *On which topics do you feel qualified to advise others?*

😀 _____

🙂 _____

117. *In which areas of your life are you completely independent?*

😀 _____

🙂 _____

118. *And in which areas do you depend on others?*

☺ ....

☺ ....

119. *If you should ever decide to write a book, what would it be about?*

☺ ....

☺ ....

120. *Do you have any special talent? Singing, drawing, etc.*

☺ ....

☺ ....

121. *And what is the talent that you wish you possessed the most?*

☺ ....

☺ ....

122. *Is there any other skill you have always wanted to learn but haven't yet? For example, learning Italian, baking cakes, etc.*

☺ ....

☺ ....

123. *If you had to be famous, what would you want to be famous for?*

☻ _____

☺ _____

124. *Who was your idol when you were a teen?*

☻ _____

☺ _____

125. *Do you have a "special place"? Why is it so meaningful to you?*

☻ _____

☺ _____

126. *If you could work in a charity, which would be and why?*

☻ _____

☺ _____

127. *Do you collaborate or have collaborated in the past with any charity?*

☻ _____

☺ _____

128. *How do you feel about social media?*

☻ _____

☺ _____

129. *How much time do you spend on social media, and how often do you post?*

😀 _____

🙂 _____

130. *Do you like to share every detail of your private life on social media, or do you prefer to keep your private life private?*

😀 _____

🙂 _____

Section 2: Favorite Things

This is a really fun section! Also, you'll find it very useful when celebrating a special occasion, choosing the perfect gift for your partner, or planning the getaway of their dreams... so don't forget to write down all your partner's answers!

131. *What's your favorite type of music?*

😀 _____

🙂 _____

132. *What's your favorite singer?*

😀 _____

🙂 _____

133. *What's your favorite group?*

☻ _____

☺ _____

134. *What's your favorite food?*

☻ _____

☺ _____

135. *What's your favorite dessert?*

☻ _____

☺ _____

136. *What's your favorite ice cream flavor?*

☻ _____

☺ _____

137. *What's your favorite drink?*

☻ _____

☺ _____

138. *What's your favorite alcoholic drink?*

☻ _____

☺ _____

139. What's your favorite fast food restaurant?

☻ --

☺ --

140. What's your favorite restaurant for casual dining?

☻ --

☺ --

141. What's your favorite restaurant for special occasions?

☻ --

☺ --

142. What's your favorite book?

☻ --

☺ --

143. What's your favorite author?

☻ --

☺ --

144. What's your favorite literary genre?

☻ --

☺ --

145. *What's your favorite movie?*

146. *What's your favorite actor/actress?*

147. *What's your favorite visual artist?*

148. *What's your favorite city in the world?*

149. *What's your favorite country?*

150. *What's your favorite color?*

151. *What's your favorite number?*

152. *What's your favorite season?*

153. *What's your favorite month of the year?*

154. *What's your favorite day of the week?*

155. *What's your favorite type of holiday?*

156. *What's your favorite pet?*

157. What's your favorite wild animal?

🙂 --

😊 --

158. What's your favorite social media?

🙂 --

😊 --

Section 3: Pets and Animals

French poet Anatole France said that "Until one has loved an animal, a part of one's soul remains unawakened." And discovering the relationship that your partner shares or shared with their beloved pet can be a great way to get an insight into their soul and the way they love. However, if this section should lead the two of you to start talking about the possibility of "parenting" a pet together, please don't forget that this is a great commitment. Animals are living and sentient beings, and caring for them requires time, attention, money, and responsibility. So, if you and your other half are at the very beginning of your love story, you might want to postpone this conversation until you're sure your relationship is stable and solid.

159. Have you ever shared your life with one or more pets?

🙂 --

😊 --

160. *Is there a pet that particularly marked your life? Why?*

☺ _____

☺ _____

161. *Are you allergic to any animals?*

☺ _____

☺ _____

162. *If your partner was allergic to your pets, would you be willing to give them away to a good home?*

☺ _____

☺ _____

163. *And if your partner didn't just like them and asked you to give them away?*

☺ _____

☺ _____

164. *Do you allow your pets to sit on the furniture, sleep in your bed, or move freely in your house?*

☺ _____

☺ _____

165. *Are there any circumstances where you think putting animals "to sleep" is the right thing to do?*

☺ _____

☺ _____

166. *Do you think pets should be spayed and neutered?*

☻ ....

☺ ....

167. *Do you think keeping a dog in a cage or tied up most of the time is cruel?*

☻ ....

☺ ....

168. *Do you think it is okay to keep birds in cages?*

☻ ....

☺ ....

169. *If you and your partner had a pet and later split up, how would you decide who the pet stays with?*

☻ ....

☺ ....

170. *Do you think pets should be bought or adopted?*

☻ ....

☺ ....

171. *If you've had pets before, where did they come from?*

☻ ....

☺ ....

172. *Do you consider that some animals should never be kept as pets or in captivity?*

☻ _____

☺ _____

173. *Do you think dogs and cats should live indoors or outdoors?*

☻ _____

☺ _____

174. *Do you take your pets with you on short trips? And long vacations?*

☻ _____

☺ _____

Section 4: The Rules of Attraction

As Emily Dickinson wrote in 1862: "The heart wants what it wants." Sometimes we don't know why we feel attracted by a particular person or why we tend to prefer brown hair and shy people over blonde hair and exuberant personalities: we just can't help ourselves from falling for that specific type. This section will help you understand a bit more what your partner is attracted to and also what they find more attractive about themselves.

175. What physical or personality traits do you think people find attractive about you?

😀 _____

🙂 _____

176. What physical or personality traits do you find more attractive when you first meet someone?

😀 _____

🙂 _____

177. Is it easy for you to find somebody attractive, or does this rarely happen?

😀 _____

🙂 _____

178. What's your partner's favorite outfit? Why?

😀 _____

🙂 _____

179. Do you like your partner's style (clothing, hairstyle, etc.)?

😀 _____

🙂 _____

180. What was the first thing that you found attractive in your partner?

😀 _____

🙂 _____

181. *How has that attraction changed since then?*

☻ _____

☺ _____

182. *Do you find the way your partner talks attractive?*

☻ _____

☺ _____

183. *Do you find the way your partner moves attractive?*

☻ _____

☺ _____

184. *What do you find attractive the most about your partner's physical features?*

☻ _____

☺ _____

185. *And what do you find attractive the most about their character?*

☻ _____

☺ _____

186. *Do you think your partner's past makes them (even more) attractive? Why?*

☻ _____

☺ _____

187. *Do you think your partner's education makes them (even more) attractive? Why?*

☻ --

☺ --

188. *Do you think your partner's job makes them (even more) attractive? Why?*

☻ --

☺ --

189. *Do you think you tend to attract a certain type of person?*

☻ --

☺ --

190. *Do you think you tend to feel attracted by a certain kind of person?*

☻ --

☺ --

191. *Do you believe in the so-called "love at first sight"?*

☻ --

☺ --

192. *Have you ever fallen in love with someone the moment you met them?*

☻ --

☺ --

193. *Have you ever dated someone you liked as a person but not that much physically?*

194. *Have you ever dated someone you liked physically but not that much as a person?*

195. *Have you ever fallen in love with someone you had known for a very long time and never romantically considered before?*

196. *Do you tend to quickly fall out of love? If yes, why do you think this happens?*

197. *Are you afraid of aging and starting to look older?*

198. Would you ever consider undergoing aesthetic surgeries to feel more comfortable with your appearance?

😊 _____

☺ _____

199. What would you think if your partner decided to have surgery of this kind?

😊 _____

☺ _____

200. Name one or two minor changes (hair, makeup, etc.) your partner could make to look even more attractive at an aesthetic level.

😊 _____

☺ _____

201. If you could change one thing only about your body, what would it be?

😊 _____

☺ _____

202. If you could change one thing only about your character, what would it be?

😊 _____

☺ _____

203. *If you were single and wanted to write a personal ad for a dating app describing your qualities, how would it read?*

☻ _____

☺ _____

Section 5: Lifestyle and Health

Some people like to go out every night, drink and eat junk food, while others prefer to exercise, sleep 8 hours per night and eat healthy all the time. And, of course, there are also a lot of "in-betweens!" The way you take care of yourself is crucial to understanding if you and your partner share similar views and goals in life, and getting to know better one another's lifestyle will allow you to talk about the compromises that you are willing to make to reach a common ground and make your relationship work.

204. *When if ever, was the first time you smoked a cigarette? Why did you try it? How long did you smoke? If you still smoke, have you ever seriously tried to quit?*

☻ _____

☺ _____

205. *Could you be in a serious relationship with someone who smokes?*

☻ _____

☺ _____

206. *If you smoke now, would you seriously attempt to quit if your partner asked you to?*

😃 ....

🙂 ....

207. *Have you ever tried recreational drugs such as marijuana? Do you still use them?*

😃 ....

🙂 ....

208. *Do you think marijuana should be made legal?*

😃 ....

🙂 ....

209. *Do you have any concerns about your health or unhealthy habits?*

😃 ....

🙂 ....

210. *Do you have any phobias, fears, or concerns about going to the doctor?*

😃 ....

🙂 ....

211. *How often do you generally get sick? Is it a cold, flu, or usually something else?*

😃 ....

🙂 ....

212. *Do you get regular medical checkups? When was your last one?*

😎 _____

☺ _____

213. *re you more likely to take over-the-counter, prescription, homeopathic, natural remedies, or nothing at all when you are sick?*

😎 _____

☺ _____

214. *Are you currently on any medication? What for?*

😎 _____

☺ _____

215. *Do you have any allergies?*

😎 _____

☺ _____

216. *Do you have any particular health concerns (e.g., heart problems, high blood pressure, diabetes, asthma, etc.)?*

😎 _____

☺ _____

217. *Do you easily get scared when you feel sick or unwell?*

😎 _____

☺ _____

218. *Do you consider yourself a hypochondriac?*

☻ ....

☺ ....

219. *Do you have any concerns over vaccinations or flu shots?*

☻ ....

☺ ....

220. *Have you ever been hospitalized? What for?*

☻ ....

☺ ....

221. *Have you ever suffered from depression? If so, why do you think it started, how long did the depression last, and what therapies worked for you?*

☻ ....

☺ ....

222. *Have you ever had an emotional breakdown? How long did the recovery take?*

☻ ....

☺ ....

223. *Have you been abused in any way - sexually, emotionally, or physically? Do you still have emotional scars from it? Have you ever been counseled about it?*

☻ ....

☺ ....

224. *Do you think your partner should take better care of their health and change some habits? Which ones?*

☺ --

☺ --

225. *Do you currently suffer from a sleeping disorder? Have you ever?*

☺ --

☺ --

226. *How many hours per night do you need to sleep to feel rested the next day?*

☺ --

☺ --

227. *How much time per day/week do you currently exercise?*

☺ --

☺ --

228. *What kind of exercise do you prefer?*

☺ --

☺ --

229. *Do you consider yourself in shape?*

☺ --

☺ --

230. *Do you have any special dietary needs?*

☻ --

☺ --

231. *Do you follow a particular diet? If yes, is it for health, ethical or religious reasons?*

☻ --

☺ --

232. *What foods do you dislike?*

☻ --

☺ --

233. *Is there any food that you could never ever eat?*

☻ --

☺ --

234. *Have you ever been on a diet to lose weight? What sort of diet?*

☻ --

☺ --

235. *Have you ever deliberately thrown up food or eaten just tiny amounts of food to lose weight?*

☻ --

☺ --

236. *Do you easily get irritated when you're hungry?*

😀 _____

🙂 _____

237. *Do you find that you eat when you are bored, stressed, or worried?*

😀 _____

🙂 _____

238. *Are there emotional times that make you want to eat?*

😀 _____

🙂 _____

239. *Do you like to plan your week's menu in advance or cook whatever you are in the mood for that day?*

😀 _____

🙂 _____

240. *Do you regularly take vitamins? Or do you consider the foods you eat to have enough vitamins in them?*

😀 _____

🙂 _____

241. *Do you try to eat healthy meals? Organic?*

😀 _____

🙂 _____

242. When grocery shopping, do you usually just buy what you need, whatever is on sale, or... is it easy for you to get "tempted"?

😃 ---

🙂 ---

243. Do you mostly cook, eat prepackaged food, or go out to eat?

😃 ---

🙂 ---

244. How many times per week do you usually dine out?

😃 ---

🙂 ---

245. Are you generally critical of the food and service when dining out?

😃 ---

🙂 ---

246. Do you feel that your table manners need improving?

😃 ---

🙂 ---

247. Do you consider that your partner's table manners could improve?

😃 ---

🙂 ---

248. *Do you consider yourself a good cook?*

☻ --

☺ --

249. *Do you enjoy cooking for other people, or do you feel you're not skilled enough?*

☻ --

☺ --

250. *When you're in a relationship, do you tend to be the one that cooks for the other person or the opposite?*

☻ --

☺ --

251. *When you're in a relationship, do you tend to be the one that goes grocery shopping or the opposite?*

☻ --

☺ --

252. *What's your favorite meal to prepare?*

☻ --

☺ --

253. *Do you eat everything on your plate, no matter how much is there? Or will you quit when you feel full? Do you need to feel "stuffed" to be satisfied?*

☻ --

☺ --

254. *What do you think about eating meals with your partner or family in front of the TV? Do you think family time and discussions around the dinner table are important?*

☻ --

☺ --

255. *Which meals of the day would you like to eat together with your partner?*

☻ --

☺ --

256. *Do you have any rooms that are off-limits for bringing in or eating food?*

☻ --

☺ --

257. *Do you enjoy eating leftovers? Or do you refuse to eat them?*

☻ --

☺ --

258. *Are you fearful of germs or food poisoning and tend to toss everything that is more than a week old out of the refrigerator?*

☻ --

☺ --

259. *Do you like to try your partner's food in restaurants?*

☺ --

☺ --

260. *Does it bother you if your partner always wants to taste your food/drink?*

☺ --

☺ --

261. *Do you consider yourself a "gourmet" - someone who enjoys trying all sorts of international cuisine, or do you prefer to eat more or less always the same food?*

☺ --

☺ --

262. *Do you drink tea and/or matcha?*

☺ --

☺ --

263. *Do you drink coffee? If so, how many times a week and how many cups each day?*

☺ --

☺ --

264. *Do you need a caffeine "fix" to get going for the day?*

☺ --

☺ --

265. *Do you remember your first alcoholic drink? And the first time you got drunk?*

☺ ....

☺ ....

266. *Generally, do you cut yourself off after a certain number of drinks? Or when do you know you have had enough?*

☺ ....

☺ ....

267. *On average, how many alcoholic beverages do you have in a week?*

☺ ....

☺ ....

268. *Do you drink (alcoholic beverages) only on the weekend are also on weekdays?*

☺ ....

☺ ....

269. *Have you ever done any dangerous things when you were drunk?*

☺ ....

☺ ....

270. *Do you ever drink and drive? Would you agree not to if that was a serious issue for your partner?*

☺ ....

☺ ....

Section 6: Holidays and Travelling

It's such a blessing to spend time with your favorite person in the world, relaxing, exploring, and discovering new cultures. But do you know what kind of holidays your partner really considers "holidays"? Find it out together and plan the perfect trip for the two of you!

271. *Have you ever traveled out of the country? Do you have a passport?*

☻ _____

☺ _____

272. *When you travel, what's your main goal (relaxing, sightseeing, seeing friends/family, discovering new cultures things, eating at new restaurants, etc.)?*

☻ _____

☺ _____

273. *Do you typically prefer to travel alone, with your partner, or with friends?*

☻ _____

☺ _____

274. *When abroad, do you enjoy experiencing different ways of life, or do you usually find it frustrating that things are not like at home?*

☻ _____

☺ _____

275. Usually, do you still attend your business while on vacation (answering email, checking voicemail, returning phone calls, etc.)?

😀 --

🙂 --

276. What's the longest vacation you have ever taken?

😀 --

🙂 --

277. If you could plan any vacation for yourself and your partner, where would it be?

😀 --

🙂 --

278. Do you prefer to travel every year to the same place or to explore a new one every time?

😀 --

🙂 --

279. Do you tend to go on "spontaneous" trips ("Hey, let's just pack and go to the mountains!")

😀 --

🙂 --

280. In which place did you spend your favorite vacation?

😀 --

🙂 --

281. *Where did you use to go as a child when on holiday?*

☻ ....

☺ ....

282. *Do you still organize trips with your parents or family?*

☻ ....

☺ ....

283. *Have you ever been on a group tour? If yes, did you enjoy the experience?*

☻ ....

☺ ....

284. *What's your favorite type of holiday?*

☻ ....

☺ ....

285. *Would you rather spend a week in a 5-star hotel or three weeks in a tent?*

☻ ....

☺ ....

286. *How much does your typical one-week vacation cost? Do you consider you take budget, moderate or expensive trips?*

☻ ....

☺ ....

287. *Do you usually save up for your vacations, or do you put everything on credit and pay it off as you go?*

☻ --

☺ --

288. *Do you generally fly as cheaply as possible, or do you choose business or first class when going on vacation?*

☻ --

☺ --

289. *Do you arrive at the airport early to avoid problems, or do you try to get there at the last minute to avoid waiting?*

☻ --

☺ --

290. *Have you ever lost a flight? If yes, what happened?*

☻ --

☺ --

291. *Have you ever taken a road trip?*

☻ --

☺ --

292. *Have you ever gone on a cruise?*

☻ --

☺ --

293. *Do you tend to get seasick or motion sick?*

☻ --

☺ --

294. *Do you like to take vacations that are activity-oriented (cycling trips, skiing trips, scuba trips, etc.)?*

☻ --

☺ --

295. *Do you enjoy going camping? What kind of eating/sleeping arrangements are tolerable for you?*

☻ --

☺ --

296. *Do you enjoy organizing weekend getaways?*

☻ --

☺ --

297. *When on holiday, do you prefer to discover your own country or travel abroad?*

☻ --

☺ --

298. When you go on a vacation with someone, do you like doing everything together, most things together, or most things on your own and then getting back together for meals?

☺ _____

☺ _____

299. Would you ever consider going on holiday with your in-laws?

☺ _____

☺ _____

300. What are your thoughts on separate vacations?

☺ _____

☺ _____

301. If you had limited income and different travel priorities, do you think you and your partner should take vacations separately every once in a while?

☺ _____

☺ _____

302. What sort of research, if any, do you do before you travel somewhere?

☺ _____

☺ _____

303. Are there any places you have no desire to go to?

😀 _____

☺ _____

304. And what are the top three places you're looking forward to visiting the most?

😀 _____

☺ _____

305. How do you handle the language barrier when you travel to foreign countries? Are you willing to visit places where your language might not be spoken?

😀 _____

☺ _____

306. Have you ever organized a surprise trip for a special person?

😀 _____

☺ _____

307. If someone should ever want to surprise you with a trip somewhere, where would you like to go?

😀 _____

☺ _____

308. *Which country/destination is the most romantic in the world for you?*

☻ ---

☺ ---

309. *Are you good at organizing your suitcase or backpack?*

☻ ---

☺ ---

310. *What do you miss the most about your home when traveling?*

☻ ---

☺ ---

311. *When on holiday, do you usually post on social media all the time, just a few pictures every now and then, or not at all?*

☻ ---

☺ ---

Section 7: Your Beliefs

We all have different beliefs, morals, and convictions. Some of us follow a particular religious code; others are taught right and wrong by their parents, and some others have developed a personal ethical code over the years. Good and bad experiences, in fact, often help us to shape our belief systems. In some cases, different viewpoints can dwell harmoniously under the same roof. Others might cause serious pain and friction. It's better to find out sooner than later, don't you think?

312. *If you and your partner had or developed opposing political views, would that affect your relationship?*

☻ _____

☺ _____

313. *Is there any particular social or political issue you would find difficult to tolerate?*

☻ _____

☺ _____

314. *Are you an activist for any causes?*

☻ _____

☺ _____

315. *Do you support (with money and/or time) any charities or causes?*

☻ _____

☺ _____

316. *Do you vote regularly?*

☻ _____

☺ _____

317. *Do you usually vote Republican, Democrat, or another party?*

☻ _____

☺ _____

318. *Or do you analyze each candidate and vote for who you think is most qualified regardless of party affiliation?*

☻ _____

☺ _____

319. *Do you have friends whose political views are different from yours?*

☻ _____

☺ _____

320. *To what extent are you involved in politics?*

☻ _____

☺ _____

321. *Is there any social cause you would physically fight for? And die?*

☻ _____

☺ _____

322. *Do you consider yourself liberal, conservative, or somewhere in the middle?*

☻ _____

☺ _____

323. *What's the biggest lie you've ever told?*

☻ _____

☺ _____

324. *Other than possible traffic violations, have you ever knowingly broken the law? If yes, what did you do?*

☺ ....

☺ ....

325. *Have you ever stolen anything?*

☺ ....

☺ ....

326. *If you found a wallet with $500 in cash, would you return it to its owner? And would you turn it in to the police if there was no identification in it?*

☺ ....

☺ ....

327. *Would you steal a car for $150,000 if you were sure that you would never get caught?*

☺ ....

☺ ....

328. *Have you ever been arrested?*

☺ ....

☺ ....

329. *What's your position on the fur industry (killing and wearing animals for fur)?*

☺ ....

☺ ....

330. What's your position on veganims?

☻ _____

☺ _____

331. What's your position on gun control?

☻ _____

☺ _____

332. What's your position on border control?

☻ _____

☺ _____

333. What's your position on the death penalty?

☻ _____

☺ _____

334. What's your position on the war in general?

☻ _____

☺ _____

335. What's your position on birth control?

☻ _____

☺ _____

336. *What's your position on abortion?*

☺ _____

☺ _____

337. *What's your position on surrogacy?*

☺ _____

☺ _____

338. *Have you ever donated your sperm or eggs? If yes, why?*

☺ _____

☺ _____

339. *Do you consider yourself a feminist?*

☺ _____

☺ _____

340. *Do you consider yourself to be a speciesist?*

☺ _____

☺ _____

341. *Do you have gay friends?*

☺ _____

☺ _____

342. How would you react if a long-time friend told you they're gay?

☻ ---

☺ ---

343. Would you date someone who is openly bisexual or who formerly was in a gay relationship?

☻ ---

☺ ---

344. Are you listed as an organ donor? Would you consider donating your organs when you die?

☻ ---

☺ ---

345. Do you think you could kill a person if they were threatening the life of your loved ones?

☻ ---

☺ ---

346. Do you think your parents are/were racist? How did that affect the way you think about people of other races?

☻ ---

☺ ---

347. Do you think your race is superior to all others/most?

☻ ---

☺ ---

348. *Generally, do you think people can learn from their mistakes and change, or will they keep repeating them?*

☺ _____

☺ _____

Section 8: Spirituality and Religion

It is definitely worth having a conversation about religion and spiritual beliefs with the person you might spend the rest of your life with, especially considering that so many people feel deeply about these topics. Please consider that, statistically, this book will be mostly purchased by Christians, and this is why an important number of the questions in this section have this specific religion in the center. In any case, feel free to make the changes that you might consider necessary to adapt one or more questions to your own spiritual beliefs.

349. *Do you believe in astrology?*

☺ _____

☺ _____

350. *Do you think your astrological birth sign represents your character?*

☺ _____

☺ _____

351. *Do you consider yourself a religious person?*

☺ _____

☺ _____

352. What were you raised to believe about religion?

☻ --
☺ --

353. Besides considering yourself a religious person, do you actually practice it?

☻ --
☺ --

354. Have you studied your religion's doctrines?

☻ --
☺ --

355. Have you read the Bible?

☻ --
☺ --

356. What are your parents' religious backgrounds?

☻ --
☺ --

357. How important is religion for your family?

☻ --
☺ --

358. *Were you afraid of God (or any other deity) as a child?*

359. *Do you currently believe in God?*

360. *Do you believe in other deities?*

361. *How does your faith help you cope with everyday problems?*

362. *Is religion important in your daily life? Why or why not?*

363. *Do you apply human logic to analyze religion? Why or why not?*

364. *What has been your worst experience with your religion or other religions?*

😊 _____

☺ _____

365. *And the most positive one?*

😊 _____

☺ _____

366. *Do you pray? How often?*

😊 _____

☺ _____

367. *If you pray, what do you generally give thanks for, and what do you ask for?*

😊 _____

☺ _____

368. *Do you go to church? How many times a week/month/year?*

😊 _____

☺ _____

369. *How many hours a week do you typically devote to your religious practices?*

😊 _____

☺ _____

370. Do you attend the church you were brought up in? Would you consider attending a different church/denomination if your partner wanted to?

😃 _____

🙂 _____

371. Can you think of anything that might make you want to stop (or start!) attending church?

😃 _____

🙂 _____

372. Do you have any religious convictions regarding sex before marriage?

😃 _____

🙂 _____

373. Does your religion have a policy on contraception? What is it?

😃 _____

🙂 _____

374. How important is religion for your when deciding to date someone seriously?

😃 _____

🙂 _____

375. What religious differences would cause you serious doubts about a long-term relationship?

☻ --

☺ --

376. Could you marry someone who does not share your fundamental religious beliefs?

☻ --

☺ --

377. Would you be willing to go through a workshop or class to understand the basic beliefs and doctrines of your partner's belief?

☻ --

☺ --

378. Do you think most people who convert to their partner's religion do so to keep the peace in the family or because they sincerely begin to understand and accept those beliefs?

☻ --

☺ --

379. Does your partner have any religious beliefs that you feel are plain wrong, and you will not be able to go along with in the long term?

☻ --

☺ --

380. *If your and your partner practice different religions, what problems do you think this might cause with your wedding, the way you celebrate holidays, and how you will raise your children?*

☻ _____

☺ _____

381. *Do you want a church wedding? If so, why?*

☻ _____

☺ _____

382. *If you and your partner currently attend the same church, but years from now, one of you stopped attending for any reason, how do you think that might affect your relationship?*

☻ _____

☺ _____

383. *Do you have any religious, ethical, or cultural reasons why you think people of different races should not marry?*

☻ _____

☺ _____

384. *If you currently do not believe, is it because of bad experiences you have had with people, or is it because you have lost faith in God?*

☻ _____

☺ _____

385. Do you have any customs or rituals regarding celebrating births and remembering deaths in your family?

😃 _____

🙂 _____

386. Do you believe in spirits, angels, or other spiritual entities?

😃 _____

🙂 _____

387. Do you believe in the existence of evil spirits? If yes, are you afraid of them?

😃 _____

🙂 _____

388. Do you believe in reincarnation?

😃 _____

🙂 _____

389. Do you believe in any sort of life after death?

😃 _____

🙂 _____

390. Are you afraid of death?

😃 _____

🙂 _____

391. *If you are a Christian, how do you feel about sharing your life with someone who does not have the same hope in eternal life?*

☻ _____

☺ _____

392. *Have you studied other faiths besides your own?*

☻ _____

☺ _____

393. *When we die, what do you think happens to us? What do you base your opinion on?*

☻ _____

☺ _____

394. *What would you like to happen to your body (buried, cremated, donated to science, etc.) when you die?*

☻ _____

☺ _____

395. *Even if you don't believe in a particular religion, do you consider yourself a spiritual person?*

☻ _____

☺ _____

396. Do you believe that humans were created with free will (the ability to make right or wrong decisions) or that everything in life is predestined?

☻ --

☺ --

397. Do you believe in any spiritual or magical practices?

☻ --

☺ --

398. What do you think about witchcraft?

☻ --

☺ --

399. Would it be okay for you to date someone who practices magical rituals?

☻ --

☺ --

400. If you have changed your mind about religion or spirituality during your life, was it because of a particular event in your life? Which one?

☻ --

☺ --

401. Do you have any superstitions? What are they?

☻ --

☺ --

Section 9: Cars and Driving

You may be wondering why I've chosen to dedicate an entire section to this topic. Well, think about it: you literally put your life in your partner's hands every time you sit in the passenger seat with them. So why not discover a bit more about their driving habits, skills, and fears? Also, for some people, their car is much more than just a vehicle; it's like their most precious possession! Let's find out if that's your or your partner's case!

402. *Do you enjoy driving?*

☻ --

☺ --

403. *What is your primary mode of transportation? Do you wish you had another option?*

☻ --

☺ --

404. *Do you generally prefer to be the driver or the passenger?*

☻ --

☺ --

405. *Do you enjoy driving on long road trips? And if you're the passenger?*

☻ --

☺ --

406. *Usually, do you find driving with your partner stressful or pleasant?*

😃 --

🙂 --

407. *Do you consider yourself a skilled driver?*

😃 --

🙂 --

408. *Do you like to drive fast?*

😃 --

🙂 --

409. *If your partner asked you to slow down or drive more carefully, would you do it?*

😃 --

🙂 --

410. *Have you ever been involved in a car crash? If yes, what happened?*

😃 --

🙂 --

411. *Have you ever received a D.U.I.? How many and how and when?*

😃 --

🙂 --

412. *Do you let other people drive your vehicle if they need one?*

☻ ....

☺ ....

413. *Is it important for you to keep your car clean, or do you allow it to pile up with trash?*

☻ ....

☺ ....

414. *Ho often do you typically wash and wax your car?*

☻ ....

☺ ....

415. *Which was your first car?*

☻ ....

☺ ....

416. *Do you tend to change your vehicle often?*

☻ ....

☺ ....

417. *What is important in a car for you (looks good, fast, five seats, reliable, good gas mileage, etc.)?*

☻ ....

☺ ....

418. *What's your favorite type of car? Do you have a favorite brand too?*

😃 _____

🙂 _____

419. *Do you ride motorcycles or other kinds of vehicles?*

😃 _____

🙂 _____

420. *Do you feel relaxed and safe when your partner is behind the wheel?*

😃 _____

🙂 _____

Section 10: Your Past and Your Future

Discovering your partner's past may help you better understand what makes them the person they are today. And knowing their aims for the future allows you to comprehend if you are moving in the same direction, and you can think about building a life together.

421. *Do you have good memories of your school years?*

😃 _____

🙂 _____

422. *Did you like studying? What was your favorite school subject?*

☻ _____

☺ _____

423. *What sports and activities did you participate in when in school?*

☻ _____

☺ _____

424. *Have you ever performed on stage in a band, a play, or another show?*

☻ _____

☺ _____

425. *Did you enjoy that kind of experience?*

☻ _____

☺ _____

426. *Did you used to go out a lot when in school or college, or did you prefer to stay at home?*

☻ _____

☺ _____

427. *Were you a responsible teenager, or did you cause your parents a lot of trouble?*

☻ _____

☺ _____

428. *Did you ever run away from home when you were younger? If yes, why?*

429. *Did you get along with your siblings while growing up?*

430. *Did you have many of friends in school? Are you still in contact with them?*

431. *Did you have a BFF in school?*

432. *Did you have a serious boyfriend or girlfriend in high school or college?*

433. *When did you fall in love for the first time?*

434. Who did you give your first kiss to?

😀 _____

🙂 _____

435. What about your "first time"?

😀 _____

🙂 _____

436. Who was your first heartbreak?

😀 _____

🙂 _____

437. Do you have any negative or traumatic memories related to dating or love during your school years?

😀 _____

🙂 _____

438. Have you ever been bullied? Or have you ever bullied someone yourself?

😀 _____

🙂 _____

439. Did you ever hang out with the wrong people in school? If yes, what kind of things did you do?

😀 _____

🙂 _____

440. *Have you ever put yourself or others in danger when you were younger?*

☻ --

☺ --

441. *Do you have any regrets when looking back at your school years?*

☻ --

☺ --

442. *Do you think you have chosen the right career, or would you do things differently if you could turn back time?*

☻ --

☺ --

443. *Have you had any serious relationships so far? How long did it last?*

☻ --

☺ --

444. *Who decided to break up? Why?*

☻ --

☺ --

445. *Are you still on good terms with this person? Do you still think about them?*

☻ --

☺ --

446. Would you like to get married someday?

☺ _____

☺ _____

447. Would you like to have children? If yes, how many?

☺ _____

☺ _____

448. Would you like to live in your current country for the rest of your life, or would you like to move abroad?

☺ _____

☺ _____

449. Is there something you would like to accomplish before you die and you haven't yet?

☺ _____

☺ _____

450. What are your top three goals for your life?

☺ _____

☺ _____

451. And what are your top three goals for this year?

☺ _____

☺ _____

452. *What steps are you actively taking to achieve these goals?*

☺ --

☺ --

453. *Where do you see yourself in five years?*

☺ --

☺ --

454. *Where do you see yourself in ten years?*

☺ --

☺ --

Section 11: Festivities and Celebrations

What are supposed to be joyful occasions way too often turn into disappointing and even tense situations. Celebrations, in fact, can imply challenging moments because of differences in cultures, traditions, and viewpoints. But even such barriers can be surmounted with the right amount of knowledge, comprehension, and effective communication.

455. *Do you like to celebrate official holidays?*

☺ --

☺ --

456. *What is your favorite holiday?*

😀 _____

🙂 _____

457. *Why is it so special to you?*

😀 _____

🙂 _____

458. *Do you like to celebrate your birthday? In a big way or more low-key?*

😀 _____

🙂 _____

459. *How did you celebrate birthdays as a child?*

😀 _____

🙂 _____

460. *Has anyone ever thrown a surprise birthday party for you?*

😀 _____

🙂 _____

461. *Have you ever done it for someone else?*

😀 _____

🙂 _____

462. *What did you do on your favorite birthday?*

☻ --

☺ --

463. *Would you like to have a bachelorette/bachelor party if you should ever get married?*

☻ --

☺ --

464. *If yes, how do you imagine it?*

☻ --

☺ --

465. *If you want to get married, how do you imagine your wedding ceremony?*

☻ --

☺ --

466. *Have you ever thought about who you would like your maid of honor/best man to be?*

☻ --

☺ --

467. *Who do you think should pay for the wedding ceremony?*

☻ --

☺ --

468. *How do you think you'll celebrate your wedding anniversary?*

☻ _____

☺ _____

469. *What are your thoughts about couples renewing their wedding vows?*

☻ _____

☺ _____

470. *How do you usually celebrate Christmas?*

☻ _____

☺ _____

471. *What's your best Christmas memory as a child?*

☻ _____

☺ _____

472. *Do you tend to buy gifts for everyone? What kind of gifts?*

☻ _____

☺ _____

473. *Do you think partners should spend the same amount on each other for Christmas?*

☻ _____

☺ _____

474. What if one of them earns more than the other?

☻ _____

☺ _____

475. In general, how much do you spend on wedding gifts? Birthday presents? Christmas gifts?

☻ _____

☺ _____

476. Do you like to use a lot of decorations for Christmas? Or nothing at all?

☻ _____

☺ _____

477. Do your religious beliefs prohibit the celebration of specific holidays?

☻ _____

☺ _____

478. Do you prefer to spend holidays like Christmas alone with your partner, with your family, or with friends?

☻ _____

☺ _____

479. How important is it for you to be with your parents at Christmas?

☻ _____

☺ _____

480. *If you have children from another relationship, how do you choose with whom they spend the holidays?*

☻ --

☺ --

481. *Do you like to host holiday parties or dinners? What do you usually do?*

☻ --

☺ --

482. *Do you tend to get emotional (irritated, sad, joyous, etc.) before or after any holidays? Which ones and why?*

☻ --

☺ --

483. *What's the best gift you could ever receive?*

☻ --

☺ --

Section 12: Home and Living Together

Dating someone is not the same as sharing your life with them on a daily basis. And it's best to discover what habits of your partner you might find irritating or incompatible with yours before moving in together. Also, you and your partner might share similar or different views about the house or city of your dreams... are you ready to find it out?

484. Where do you think you would be most comfortable living? Big city or small town in the countryside? Flat or house?

485. Would you prefer to live close to the beach or the mountains?

486. Would you rather live in a place with a very hot or very cold climate?

487. Would you ever consider moving abroad? If yes, to which country?

488. Is there any country you would refuse to live in?

489. *Do you dream about living in a place in particular? Which one?*

☻ _____

☺ _____

490. *Have you ever lived abroad? If yes, where?*

☻ _____

☺ _____

491. *Would you rather move often and experience life in different places or stay in the same place for your entire life?*

☻ _____

☺ _____

492. *At what age did you leave your parents' home?*

☻ _____

☺ _____

493. *What did you like the most about the house where you grew up? And the least?*

☻ _____

☺ _____

494. *What did you like the most about the city/town where you grew up? And the least?*

☻ _____

☺ _____

495. Have you ever lived with a boyfriend/girlfriend?

😃 --

😊 --

496. If yes, was this a positive or negative experience, and why?

😃 --

😊 --

497. Can you describe your dream home?

😃 --

😊 --

498. What's the number one thing that couldn't be missing in your dream home?

😃 --

😊 --

499. And how do you envision your home (your realistic home - not your dream home)? The architecture, the décor, the garden, etc.?

😃 --

😊 --

500. Do you enjoy decorating your home?

😃 --

😊 --

501. *What decoration style do you like the most? Vintage, minimalist, country, extravagant, etc.*

😃 _____

🙂 _____

502. *Would you rather buy a brand new place or a place to renovate according to your own taste?*

😃 _____

🙂 _____

503. *What's your favorite part of the house?*

😃 _____

🙂 _____

504. *What would you change about your current home?*

😃 _____

🙂 _____

505. *If you have a yard at home, how many hours per week do you usually spend taking care of it?*

😃 _____

🙂 _____

506. *Do you prefer a low-maintenance yard or a style that demands a bit of work?*

😃 _____

🙂 _____

507. *Do you enjoy gardening? Do you expect your partner to help you with this kind of work?*

☻ --

☺ --

508. *What's the housework you dislike the most?*

☻ --

☺ --

509. *And the one you actually enjoy?*

☻ --

☺ --

510. *Do you consider yourself an untidy or tidy person?*

☻ --

☺ --

511. *Do you clean up the kitchen after every meal? Each night? Or when you run out of dishes or company is coming over?*

☻ --

☺ --

512. *Do you usually put things back where they belong soon after you use them?*

☻ --

☺ --

513. *How clean do you keep your house?*

☺ _____

☺ _____

514. *From 1 to 10, how important is it for you to live in a clean and tidy house?*

☺ _____

☺ _____

515. *How often do you consider the sheets should be changed?*

☺ _____

☺ _____

516. *Do you declutter often, or do you tend to accumulate things and stuff at home?*

☺ _____

☺ _____

517. *Are you a handy person? Do you take care of fixing things yourself?*

☺ _____

☺ _____

518. *Do you enjoy DIY projects?*

☺ _____

☺ _____

519. *Do you usually listen to music around the house? What kind? How loud?*

😃 --

🙂 --

520. *What temperature do you like in the house during winter? And in summer?*

😃 --

🙂 --

521. *Do you allow people to smoke in your house?*

😃 --

🙂 --

522. *How long does it take for you to get ready in the morning?*

😃 --

🙂 --

523. *And how long does it take to get ready for bed?*

😃 --

🙂 --

524. *What are your sleeping habits?*

😃 --

🙂 --

525. *Are you able to fall asleep with the lights on? With the TV or radio on?*

☻ _____

☺ _____

526. *Do you snore? Could someone hear you snoring from another room?*

☻ _____

☺ _____

527. *Do you like to sleep hugging your partner or on your side of the bed?*

☻ _____

☺ _____

528. *How do you feel about your partner using your toothbrush?*

☻ _____

☺ _____

529. *Do you prefer to shower in the morning or before going to bed?*

☻ _____

☺ _____

530. *How many times a day do you brush your teeth?*

☻ _____

☺ _____

531. *Do you make your bed every day?*

☻ ---

☺ ---

532. *When taking off your clothes, do you immediately put them in the washer if dirty, hang them up or fold them if clean, or leave them on the floor?*

☻ ---

☺ ---

533. *Do you make your bed every day?*

☻ ---

☺ ---

534. *Does it bother you if it is left unmade?*

☻ ---

☺ ---

535. *What time do you usually go to bed during the week?*

☻ ---

☺ ---

536. *What about weekends?*

☻ ---

☺ ---

537. *Do you expect both you and your partner to go to bed at the same time?*

☻ ....

☺ ....

538. *How would you feel if your partner often wanted to stay up more or go to sleep before you?*

☻ ....

☺ ....

Section 13: Hobbies and Free Time

Most of us have a very busy lifestyle and not much time left for our hobbies and favorite activities. Finding out how your partner likes to spend their free time will help you better understand what kind of activities you can do together and how much you'll need to compromise...

539. *If you could take a paid sabbatical year, what would you most like to do?*

☻ ....

☺ ....

540. *Do you prefer to spend your weekends at home, going out with friends, or being productive?*

☻ ....

☺ ....

541. *What sort of parties do you enjoy going to?*

☻ _____

☺ _____

542. *When going to a party, do you like to go for a short while or stay until most people have gone?*

☻ _____

☺ _____

543. *Do you enjoy going to amusement parks?*

☻ _____

☺ _____

544. *Do you like thrill rides too?*

☻ _____

☺ _____

545. *Do you often go to musicals, operas, or plays? If not, why?*

☻ _____

☺ _____

546. *Do you enjoy going to concerts or music festivals?*

☻ _____

☺ _____

547. *How often do you attend events of this kind?*

☺ _____

☺ _____

548. *Do you prefer watching a movie on the big screen or on Netflix?*

☺ _____

☺ _____

549. *Do you have a specific location in the movie theater where you prefer to sit?*

☺ _____

☺ _____

550. *Do you prefer movies or series?*

☺ _____

☺ _____

551. *What do you enjoy the most: reading a book or watching a movie/series?*

☺ _____

☺ _____

552. *Which are your three favorite series?*

☺ _____

☺ _____

553. Which are your three favorite movies?

☻ --

☺ --

554. Which is your favorite TV show (talk show, cooking show, etc.)?

☻ --

☺ --

555. Which are your three favorite books?

☻ --

☺ --

556. How many books do you typically read in a year?

☻ --

☺ --

557. What type of books do you read?

☻ --

☺ --

558. Do you prefer reading your books as paperbacks or e-books?

☻ --

☺ --

559. *Do you usually spend time in the library?*

☻ _____

☺ _____

560. *Which newspapers do you generally read?*

☻ _____

☺ _____

561. *How often do you watch the news?*

☻ _____

☺ _____

562. *Do you spend a lot of time watching TV?*

☻ _____

☺ _____

563. *Do you spend a lot of time playing video games?*

☻ _____

☺ _____

564. *Do you collect anything? If yes, how much do you spend each year on your collections?*

☻ _____

☺ _____

565. What role does art play in your life?

566. What is your favorite type of art?

567. Do you like drawing or painting?

568. Do you have any particular hobbies?

569. Are you a fan of any sport in particular? How often do you go watch your team play?

570. How personally involved do you get with "your" team's performance?

571. *If your team loses, do you get mad?*

☺ ....

☺ ....

572. *How many sports have you played in your life?*

☺ ....

☺ ....

573. *Do you prefer to go to the gym or play an "actual" sport?*

☺ ....

☺ ....

574. *Who is your favorite player (no matter the sport) of all time?*

☺ ....

☺ ....

575. *How much time do you spend scrolling on social media?*

☺ ....

☺ ....

576. *Do you like playing cards? Are you good at it?*

☺ ....

☺ ....

577. What games do you enjoy the most?

😃 _____

😊 _____

578. Do you consider yourself a competitive person?

😃 _____

😊 _____

579. If your partner had a great interest in a sport or activity that you had absolutely no liking or interest in, would you be willing to give it a try?

😃 _____

😊 _____

580. And if your partner didn't like your hobby, would you consider doing less of what you like to enjoy more time with your other half?

😃 _____

😊 _____

581. Do you enjoy going shopping? How often do you go?

😃 _____

😊 _____

582. Are you a big spender?

😃 _____

😊 _____

583. *On what items do you spend the most (clothes, accessories, skincare, electronics, books, video games, travels, etc.)?*

☻ ....

☺ ....

584. *How often do you treat yourself to a spa or massage? Is this a kind of activity you like to enjoy with your partner?*

☻ ....

☺ ....

585. *Which are the three activities that relax you the most in the world?*

☻ ....

☺ ....

Section 14: Relationships and Dating Life

When you ask, "What's your definition of love?" it's hard to find two people who will give you the exact same answer. However, it's crucial that you and your other half speak the same language and share the same values on this topic. And that both of you are well aware of the fact that keeping the flame alive requires some serious work...

586. *Do you believe in the romantic idea of love?*

☻ ....

☺ ....

587. *Do you consider yourself a romantic person? Why?*

☺ _____

☺ _____

588. *Do you consider your partner romantic?*

☺ _____

☺ _____

589. *Which is the craziest thing you've ever done in the name of love?*

☺ _____

☺ _____

590. *Do you tend to be affectionate to your partner in front of other people?*

☺ _____

☺ _____

591. *What kind of physical affection do you think is appropriate in public?*

☺ _____

☺ _____

592. *Has your partner done things that make you question whether or not they love you?*

☺ _____

☺ _____

593. *Is there anything your partner could do to make you feel more loved/appreciated?*

😃 --

🙂 --

594. *Can you name three things your partner has done for you that made you feel loved?*

😃 --

🙂 --

595. *Have you ever written a love letter?*

😃 --

🙂 --

596. *Have you ever received one? How did that make you feel?*

😃 --

🙂 --

597. *What's your ideal date?*

😃 --

🙂 --

598. *What did you think after the first date with your current partner?*

😃 --

🙂 --

599. *On that day/night, did you wish for things to get serious between the two of you? Or did it happen later?*

😀 ....

☺ ....

600. *What was the best date you and your current partner have been on?*

😀 ....

☺ ....

601. *How do you tend to express your love to your partner (gifts, compliments, helping them out, etc.)?*

😀 ....

☺ ....

602. *And in which ways you like to be shown that someone loves you?*

😀 ....

☺ ....

603. *Is it difficult for you to say "I love you"? If yes, why?*

😀 ....

☺ ....

604. *Do you need your partner to tell you "I love you" or similar words on a regular basis?*

😀 ....

☺ ....

605. *Have you been married before?*

☻ --

☺ --

606. *If yes, would you consider marrying again?*

☻ --

☺ --

607. *Would you consider marrying someone who was previously married? Or would that be a problem for you in any way?*

☻ --

☺ --

608. *Have you ever loved two people at the same time?*

☻ --

☺ --

609. *Do you believe in polyamory? Have you ever been in a relationship of this kind, or would you be willing to accept it?*

☻ --

☺ --

610. *Do you believe or would you be willing to be in an open relationship?*

☻ --

☺ --

611. *Have you ever been in love or felt attracted by someone of your same sex?*

😃 ....

☺ ....

612. *Have you ever been unfaithful?*

😃 ....

☺ ....

613. *To your knowledge, have you ever been cheated on? How did you react?*

😃 ....

☺ ....

614. *Do you believe true love lasts a lifetime or that it inevitably fades away?*

😃 ....

☺ ....

615. *Do you think that love is enough? Or that two very different persons won't be able to make it work no matter how much they love one another?*

😃 ....

☺ ....

616. *What is the number one thing you could never forgive your partner?*

😃 ....

☺ ....

617. *What rituals could be added to your current relationship daily, weekly, monthly, and yearly to help the two of you remain close?*

☻ _____

☺ _____

Section 15: Family and Friends

Both family and friends have the power to bring people together... but also to drive them apart. When you decide to share your life with another person, some adjustments usually need to be made in this sense, and a lot of communication is necessary to continue to have a good relationship with friends and relatives. Once again, knowing more about the most important persons in your partner's life can be of great help!

618. *How do you feel about the way your parents raised you? Do you think they did a good job, or they messed it up?*

☻ _____

☺ _____

619. *Are there things you would do it differently if you had children of your own?*

☻ _____

☺ _____

620. *Do you think your family has been a poor or good relationship model?*

☻ _____

☺ _____

621. *What positive things have you learned from observing your parents' marriage?*

☻ _____

☺ _____

622. *As of today, what's your parents' relationship like? Do they still love each other?*

☻ _____

☺ _____

623. *In your opinion, what makes the difference between a good parent and a great parent?*

☻ _____

☺ _____

624. *What did you enjoy doing the most with your family as a kid?*

☻ _____

☺ _____

625. *What's your current relationship with your parents?*

☻ _____

☺ _____

626. *How often do you see your family? Do you think that's enough?*

☻ _____

☺ _____

627. *And how often do you call your parents/family members?*

☻ _____

☺ _____

628. *What is the most important thing you learned from your father?*

☻ _____

☺ _____

629. *What is the most important thing you learned from your mother?*

☻ _____

☺ _____

630. *Did you ever hear or see your parents fighting when you were a child? How did that make you feel?*

☻ _____

☺ _____

631. *What's the biggest fight you've had with your family? Has the issue been settled?*

☻ --

☺ --

632. *As of today, which family member are you closest to? Has it always been that way?*

☻ --

☺ --

633. *Are your grandparents still alive?*

☻ --

☺ --

634. *If yes, do you have a close relationship with them?*

☻ --

☺ --

635. *Do you have a favorite relative? What makes them so special to you?*

☻ --

☺ --

636. *Do you have a big family that gets together often? Or is it the opposite?*

☻ --

☺ --

637. *Do you feel obligated to keep close family ties with relatives you would not normally choose to socialize with? Do you consider it appropriate to "divorce" from family members?*

😃 _____

🙂 _____

638. *On a scale from 1 to 10, how is your family important to you?*

😃 _____

🙂 _____

639. *Do you think you could live more than six hours away from your parents and/or siblings?*

😃 _____

🙂 _____

640. *If your family disliked your partner and asked you to break up with/not marry them, how much could their opinion influence you?*

😃 _____

🙂 _____

641. *Early in the dating stage, how strongly do you consider your friends and family's opinion on whether you should continue seeing that person?*

😃 _____

🙂 _____

642. Can you say "no" to your parents when they want you to do something you would prefer not to?

☻ --

☺ --

643. Have you ever thought about how you will take care of your mom and dad when they are older and need assistance?

☻ --

☺ --

644. Did you grow up in an ethnic or culturally unique community? What role did that play in your life?

☻ --

☺ --

645. What is your parents' nationality? Were you raised in that culture, or do you know much about it?

☻ --

☺ --

646. Did you have any special family traditions while growing up? Would you want your children to continue them?

☻ --

☺ --

647. *If you had children, how often would you like them to see their grandparents?*

☺ _____

☺ _____

648. *Would you have any particular concern about them spending too much time with any of their grandparents or relatives?*

☺ _____

☺ _____

649. *Do you think your parents will help you when and if you decide to have children?*

☺ _____

☺ _____

650. *What would you say if a friend or relative asked you to live in your house for a year?*

☺ _____

☺ _____

651. *Do you like it when relatives or friends feel comfortable enough to drop by your house unexpectedly?*

☺ _____

☺ _____

652. What do you think is the main thing you and your (or at least most) friends have in common (school, work, sport, music, etc.)?

☻ --

☺ --

653. Do you enjoy hosting out-of-town friends or relatives in your home? If so, for how long?

☻ --

☺ --

654. 654 Is it hard for you to let old friends "go" when you realize you have little or nothing yet in common?

☻ --

☺ --

655. On a typical day/night out with your friends, what do you like to do?

☻ --

☺ --

656. Are you still friends with your high school classmates?

☻ --

☺ --

657. How long have you been friends with the friend you have known for the longest time?

☻ --

☺ --

658. *How did you meet your current best friend?*

☻ _____

☺ _____

659. *Why do you consider them your best friend?*

☻ _____

☺ _____

660. *What kind of betrayal could you never forgive a friend?*

☻ _____

☺ _____

661. *Have you ever fought with a friend over a love interest?*

☻ _____

☺ _____

662. *Do you have good friends of the opposite sex?*

☻ _____

☺ _____

663. *How do you feel about your partner having close friends of the opposite sex?*

☻ _____

☺ _____

664. When you are in a serious relationship, do you tend to ignore or see your friends less?

☻ --

☺ --

665. Have you had friends that got married and suddenly lost contact with their single friends? Is that to be expected?

☻ --

☺ --

666. Which of your friends do you consider the most successful? Would you like to have the same level of success?

☻ --

☺ --

667. Do any of your friends have things that make you feel envious?

☻ --

☺ --

668. Do you think you are a good or a bad influence on your friends?

☻ --

☺ --

669. *Do you think your friends are a good or a bad influence on you?*

😃 ....

🙂 ....

670. *How powerful is peer pressure on you? Do you feel you need to live similarly to your friends?*

😃 ....

🙂 ....

671. *If you should ever get married, do you think there would be any changes in your social circle?*

😃 ....

🙂 ....

672. *Three essential ingredients for a healthy friendship?*

😃 ....

🙂 ....

673. *Are you currently satisfied with the quality and quantity of friends you have? Why or why not?*

😃 ....

🙂 ....

674. *What's the song that makes you think about your friends?*

😃 ....

🙂 ....

675. *If you were married, how would you like to meet new people to socialize with?*

☺ --

☺ --

676. *Do you like your partner's friends? Why or why not?*

☺ --

☺ --

Section 16: Communication

If your partner has agreed to answer all these questions with you, that's already a great sign that they value communication and know how important it is in a relationship. But there's more you can do to make things work between the two of you: for example, understanding why they communicate the way they do and finding out how they would like you to say things to them.

677. *Do you think you and your current partner communicate in a healthy way?*

☺ --

☺ --

678. *Have you ever felt like you don't know your partner at all? If yes, which "gaps" do you think need to be filled?*

☺ --

☺ --

679. *Is there anything you don't like about your partner's way of communicating with you?*

☻ ....

☺ ....

680. *If you are in a bad mood, should your partner leave you alone, encourage you to talk, or do something else?*

☻ ....

☺ ....

681. *Are there things that are easier for you to discuss with your friends than with your partner?*

☻ ....

☺ ....

682. *Do you think you're good at reading your partner's body language?*

☻ ....

☺ ....

683. *And do you think your partner can read your own body language?*

☻ ....

☺ ....

684. *Are there any things of a couple's private life that should not be discussed with family or friends?*

☻ _____

☺ _____

685. *Do you think your partner can listen to you and do something else (like watching TV or reading the paper) at the same time? Can you?*

☻ _____

☺ _____

686. *Do you think your partner talks too much on the phone? Or a little too much in general?*

☻ _____

☺ _____

687. *Do you think that your partner often takes ten minutes to tell you something that could have been said in 30 seconds? How do you feel about it?*

☻ _____

☺ _____

688. *If your partner should get offended or irritated at something you say or do, what is the best way for them to bring it up to you without hurting your feelings?*

☻ _____

☺ _____

689. *Do you think it is okay for someone to correct their partner in public?*

690. *Do you find it easy to start conversations with strangers?*

691. *Are you good at small talk?*

692. *Can you have meaningful conversations with someone you were just introduced to?*

693. *When you really don't feel like talking to your partner, why is it generally that?*

694. *Do you prefer to stay in touch with friends and family by phone, WhatsApp, email, Instagram, etc.?*

695. Do you usually return phone calls and messages on the same day?

☻ --

☺ --

696. Do you have many friends living abroad? Are you good at keeping your friendships alive despite the distance?

☻ --

☺ --

697. Can you accept that some things from your partner's past might be too painful for them to share even with you?

☻ --

☺ --

698. Would you be able to commit to someone who can't share everything?

☻ --

☺ --

699. Do you think your partner tends to interrupt your sentences or monopolize the conversation? If yes, do you find it irritating?

☻ --

☺ --

700. *Do you consider you like to talk about yourself - your job, your vacations, your accomplishments, etc.?*

😃 ....

☺ ....

701. *Do you feel that others may think that you talk too much about yourself?*

😃 ....

☺ ....

702. *Do you think your partner likes to talk about themselves?*

😃 ....

☺ ....

703. *After a fight, do you like to settle things by talking about what happened, or do you need some time and space?*

😃 ....

☺ ....

704. *Do you like to talk about your feelings and emotions, or is it something difficult for you?*

😃 ....

☺ ....

705. *Did your family tend to share feelings and emotions when you were growing up?*

☺ --

☺ --

706. *In what areas do you think you and your partner could most improve your communication?*

☺ --

☺ --

707. *Is there any topic you wish you and your partner could discuss more openly and freely?*

☺ --

☺ --

708. *And is there any topic you just don't like or feel really uncomfortable talking about?*

☺ --

☺ --

Section 17: Education and Career

You may have already achieved all your professional goals, or you may be struggling to understand what you want to do in life. You might have studied the career of your dreams, or you might have chosen a path marked by your family. No matter your situation, having a partner who is there for you and supports your professional objectives is basic to building a lasting and happy union.

709. *Do you think you could ever leave your current life and move to another city or country for your dream job?*

😀 --

🙂 --

710. *Could you do it for your partner's dream job?*

😀 --

🙂 --

711. *Is your current job your dream job?*

😀 --

🙂 --

712. *On a scale from 1 to 10, how satisfied you're with your current job?*

😀 --

🙂 --

713. *What are your career goals 5, 10, and 20 years from now?*

😀 --

🙂 --

714. *When you were a child, what did you want to be when you grew up?*

😀 --

🙂 --

715. What is the best job you ever had? Why was it?

☻ _____

☺ _____

716. Do you consider yourself a hard-working person?

☻ _____

☺ _____

717. If you have a boss, how happy are you with them?

☻ _____

☺ _____

718. Have you ever gone to your boss and asked for a raise? How did it go?

☻ _____

☺ _____

719. If you have co-workers, how happy are you with them?

☻ _____

☺ _____

720. Would you prefer to work in a big international company, in a small charity, or as an independent freelance?

☻ _____

☺ _____

721. *Do you prefer working from home or in a place where you can interact with others?*

☻ _____

☺ _____

722. *Do you work well under stress?*

☻ _____

☺ _____

723. *Do you work better alone or with a team? Why?*

☻ _____

☺ _____

724. *Have you ever dated a colleague at work? Did the company have a policy against that?*

☻ _____

☺ _____

725. *How often do you call in sick when you are not really ill?*

☻ _____

☺ _____

726. *Do you often take your job home with you?*

☻ _____

☺ _____

727. In your present career, how much do you think you will be making in 3 years? 10 years?

☻ ....

☺ ....

728. Have you ever felt that a promotion was given to someone else when you were much more deserving? How did you handle it?

☻ ....

☺ ....

729. How many hours do you currently work per week? Do you think that will change the day you'll have a family to come home to?

☻ ....

☺ ....

730. Do you feel like your job allows you to make a difference somehow?

☻ ....

☺ ....

731. Do you have a role model in your profession? What do you admire in them?

☻ ....

☺ ....

732. Do you think you would ever have an interest in running for a political office?

☻ ....

☺ ....

733. Would you take a job that paid you 70% of your current salary, but gave you 100% job satisfaction?

☻ ....

☺ ....

734. If someone wanted to finance the startup of your business with no strings attached, what business would you start?

☻ ....

☺ ....

735. How do you feel about mixing business with family? Business with friends? Do you have any experience in this sense?

☻ ....

☺ ....

736. At what age or what level of financial stability would you like to retire? How do you think you would spend your retirement?

☻ ....

☺ ....

737. Are you already working on your retirement plan?

☻ --

☺ --

738. Would you rather choose a job that doesn't pay too much but gives you the freedom of working from any place in the world at any time or a very well-paid job that requires you to go to the office every day?

☻ --

☺ --

739. Would you ever work as an influencer or YouTuber and expose your life to other people?

☻ --

☺ --

740. What changes do you think your partner would need to make to feel satisfied on a career level?

☻ --

☺ --

741. Would it ever be okay or desirable that you or your partner didn't work?

☻ --

☺ --

742. *How important is it for you to have a hard-working and financially independent partner?*

☺ --

☺ --

743. *Did you go to college? Where? What degree(s) did you get if any?*

☺ --

☺ --

744. *Do you think your education has paid off? How?*

☺ --

☺ --

745. *How did you choose your major in college?*

☺ --

☺ --

746. *If you could turn back time, would you choose a different path?*

☺ --

☺ --

747. *Have you ever thought about starting to study again? If yes, what would you like to study?*

☺ --

☺ --

Section 18: It's all About the Money

Disagreements over money are one of the leading causes of divorce for couples in the United States. That's why you'll have to agree with me when I say that knowing your partner's ideas and plans on this subject is something essential. After all, if you dream of living a simple life, enjoying your free time and working as little as possible, and your other half's ultimate goal is to buy a yacht in less than five years, you're probably going to have to make some adjustments...

748. If a late parent left you $200,000 in their will with the stipulation that you had to invest it for 15 years before you could touch it, how would you invest the money?

😃 ....

🙂 ....

749. And if you inherited $200,000 to spend as you like, how would you use the money?

😃 ....

🙂 ....

750. Do you easily get stressed out when finances are tight?

😃 ....

🙂 ....

751. Do you have self-control and only spend what you can pay off each month?

😃 ....

🙂 ....

752. *Do you like to buy luxury items, or are you frugal with your money?*

☻ _____

☺ _____

753. *How many credit cards are there in your wallet?*

☻ _____

☺ _____

754. *Have you ever invested in cryptocurrencies?*

☻ _____

☺ _____

755. *Do you have money invested in the stock market?*

☻ _____

☺ _____

756. *Have you ever gotten a second job to help pay for your nonessential (or essential) purchases?*

☻ _____

☺ _____

757. *Did you complete your taxes from this previous year? Do you always file on time?*

☻ _____

☺ _____

758. *Have you ever filed for bankruptcy?*

☻ _____

☺ _____

759. *Does your income cover all your expenses every month?*

☻ _____

☺ _____

760. *Can you save money every month?*

☻ _____

☺ _____

761. *How many months of expenses do you think you should have in savings to feel secure?*

☻ _____

☺ _____

762. *If you don't already have that much, how do you plan on building up your savings?*

☻ _____

☺ _____

763. *In which category (housing, clothing, food, entertainment, skincare, etc.) do you think you should cut back the most to achieve your goals?*

☻ _____

☺ _____

764. *Do you think you have ever been "used" for money?*

☺ _____

☺ _____

765. *Have you ever supported a partner financially?*

☺ _____

☺ _____

766. *Have you ever felt that a partner didn't respect your hard-earned income by how they spent it?*

☺ _____

☺ _____

767. *Do you think partners should keep their money in joint or individual accounts? Why?*

☺ _____

☺ _____

768. *Have you ever loaned a large sum of money to someone? Would you do it again?*

☺ _____

☺ _____

769. *Have you ever been loaned a large sum of money? Have you paid it back?*

☺ _____

☺ _____

770. *Do you think lending significant amounts of money to boyfriends/girlfriends is wise? Have you ever done such a thing?*

☻ _____

☺ _____

771. *Do you think financially supporting your partner while they care for the house and children is the best choice for a family?*

☻ _____

☺ _____

772. *If your spouse wanted to quit work to go back to school, write a novel, or do something else that would imply making no money, would you support them? For how long?*

☻ _____

☺ _____

773. *What problems do you see with the "my money, your money" approach to finances in a marriage?*

☻ _____

☺ _____

774. *Do you think your partner takes care of their money in a responsible way?*

☻ _____

☺ _____

775. *Could you seriously date someone whom you really like and who is great in many ways but terrible at managing their money?*

☻ _____

☺ _____

776. *If you were dating someone who had a lot of debts, how would you feel about helping them pay them off?*

☻ _____

☺ _____

777. *How much debt do you think a couple should take within the first year or two of marriage, given that financial problems are one of the leading causes of divorce?*

☻ _____

☺ _____

778. *How do you think a couple should decide to spend their money? Each partner should feel free to spend whatever they want as long as it's "their money," or is there an amount ($100, $500, $1,000) at which they should discuss the purchase with their other half?*

☻ _____

☺ _____

779. *Do you think your and your partner's families have the right to know your financial situation in detail?*

☻ _____

☺ _____

780. What would you tell them if they asked how much money you and your partner make or how much money you have in the bank?

☻ _____

☺ _____

781. If you got into financial difficulties, how would you try to get out of it?

☻ _____

☺ _____

782. If your partner thought you needed help keeping your finances under control and suggested a "debt counselor," would you agree to go?

☻ _____

☺ _____

783. Considering that nearly 50% of marriages in the U.S. end in divorce, do you think a prenuptial agreement indicates a lack of trust, or is it a wise act to protect what you have worked for? What do you think would be fair in terms of the agreement?

☻ _____

☺ _____

784. Have you ever dated someone just because they had (or you thought they had) money?

☻ _____

☺ _____

785. *If you and your partner's income doubled, how would you like your lifestyle to change?*

☻ _____

☺ _____

786. *If you began to make significantly more money, would you like to move into a bigger/fancier house?*

☻ _____

☺ _____

787. *At what point would you consider yourself "rich"?*

☻ _____

☺ _____

788. *If you were single and fairly well off, how would you sort out "gold-diggers"?*

☻ _____

☺ _____

789. *What's your dream car? How much money would you have to make to justify that expense?*

☻ _____

☺ _____

790. *When two people go on a date, who do you think should pay? Whoever arranged it? Whoever makes the most money? Always Dutch? Some other arrangement?*

☻ _____

☺ _____

791. *What sort of tipper are you? Always 15%? Or more or less depending on the service?*

☻ ....

☺ ....

792. *Would you ever spend $200 on a bottle of wine? $300? Under what circumstances?*

☻ ....

☺ ....

793. *What is the minimum amount you think you should spend on your wedding day?*

☻ ....

☺ ....

794. *Would you rather live modestly and retire modestly at 50, or would you rather live a more expensive lifestyle and retire modestly at 65?*

☻ ....

☺ ....

795. *Would you rather live modestly doing what you love or gain a lot of money doing something you don't like?*

☻ ....

☺ ....

796. *Do you have health insurance?*

☻ ....

☺ ....

797. *Do you think life insurance is a wise "investment"?*

798. *How much (percentage of income) do you think a person should give to a church or charity?*

799. *Do you currently have a will? If not, why?*

800. *Do you think you tend to obsess over money?*

801. *Between you and your partner, who has the best skills at paying the bills and keeping track of the expenses?*

802. *Which of you has the best skills for investing money?*

Section 19: Past and Present Relationships

The romantic past of your partner can tell you a lot about how they are and behave in a relationship. For example, if your better half has cheated on all their previous partners and has no regrets, this could indicate some sort of red flag, don't you think? However, some people need to find the love of their love to start behaving responsibly and maturely in a relationship, and others might be acting in a certain way because they have been hurt in the past. In any case, finding out more about your partner's past relationships (and what they want from their current one) can help your future as a couple. Just keep in mind to avoid asking or giving graphic details if you don't want to run the risk of hurting each other!

803. *What do/did you most enjoy about being single?*

☻ --

☺ --

804. *784 What do/did you dislike the most about being single?*

☻ --

☺ --

805. *What do you enjoy the most about being in a relationship?*

☻ --

☺ --

806. *And what do you dislike the most about being in a relationship?*

☻ _____

☺ _____

807. *Do you enjoy flirting with others? Why?*

☻ _____

☺ _____

808. *When in a relationship, do you tend to miss flirting with new people?*

☻ _____

☺ _____

809. *Do you think it is a good idea to casually date more than one person at a time?*

☻ _____

☺ _____

810. *What's the maximum number of people you've ever dated simultaneously?*

☻ _____

☺ _____

811. *At what point do you feel it is necessary to date only one person exclusively?*

☻ _____

☺ _____

812. *Do you consider yourself a "serial dater"? Have you ever been one at some point in your life?*

☺ --

☺ --

813. *When you were single, did you have rules about seeing people who were already involved with someone?*

☺ --

☺ --

814. *Have you ever dated or slept with a friend's partner, former partner or love interest?*

☺ --

☺ --

815. *As a general rule, do you always (or never) kiss on a first date?*

☺ --

☺ --

816. *And how long do you think it's wise to wait before going to bed with someone? Or do you think there's no need to wait at all?*

☺ --

☺ --

817. *Do you think you have dated enough people to know for sure when a great match comes along?*

☻ --

☺ --

818. *How long do you think most people can "be on their best behavior" and hide their authentic selves while dating?*

☻ --

☺ --

819. *Have you tended to date people older or younger than you? Do you think there's a reason for that?*

☻ --

☺ --

820. *Could you date someone who is 20 years younger than you?*

☻ --

☺ --

821. *Could you date someone who is 20 years older than you?*

☻ --

☺ --

822. *Have you mostly dated people who have similar physical characteristics? What are they?*

☺ --

☺ --

823. *Who is your all-time celebrity crush?*

☺ --

☺ --

824. *What's the number one thing you look for in a life partner?*

☺ --

☺ --

825. *Do you think it is generally better to be friends with someone before having a relationship with them?*

☺ --

☺ --

826. *And do you think two former lovers can build up (or re-build) a real friendship after splitting up?*

☺ --

☺ --

827. *How did you meet your former partners?*

☺ --

☺ --

828. *How many times have you fallen in love?*

☻ ....

☺ ....

829. *Do you think it's true that you will never forget your first love?*

☻ ....

☺ ....

830. *How many people have you said "I Love You" to?*

☻ ....

☺ ....

831. *How long do you think is it wise to wait to tell someone you love them?*

☻ ....

☺ ....

832. *Have you ever secretly been in love with someone and not told them how you felt? If yes, why?*

☻ ....

☺ ....

833. *Have you ever been in love with someone who was married/in a serious relationship with someone else? If yes, what did you do?*

☻ ....

☺ ....

834. Has anyone who was married/in a serious relationship ever asked you out? What did you do?

🙂 _____

🙂 _____

835. Have you ever thought you were in love and realized you were only infatuated?

🙂 _____

🙂 _____

836. How long did it take for you to realize it wasn't real love?

🙂 _____

🙂 _____

837. How many serious relationships have you been in?

🙂 _____

🙂 _____

838. Why things ended?

🙂 _____

🙂 _____

839. How long did your longest relationship last? Do you regret staying in it that long?

🙂 _____

🙂 _____

840. *What did your previous partners complain the most about you?*

841. *Do you think you have a "type" and always tend to fall for the same kind of person?*

842. *In normal circumstances, how long do you think a couple should date or live together to know each other well enough to get engaged?*

843. *If your partner should sleep with someone else, would that automatically mean the end of the relationship for you?*

844. *Is it hard for you to end a relationship because you don't want to hurt the other person?*

845. In past relationships, have you ever played games? How so?

😃 --

😊 --

846. What is the worst thing that a former partner has ever done to you?

😃 --

😊 --

847. What bothered you the most about your previous partners?

😃 --

😊 --

848. Have you ever gotten some kind of revenge on your previous partners? How?

😃 --

😊 --

849. Have you ever "ghosted" anyone?

😃 --

😊 --

850. Have you ever been "ghosted"? How did that make you feel?

😃 --

😊 --

851. *Have you ever been in a strictly online relationship?*

😃 _____

🙂 _____

852. *Have you ever been "catfished"?*

😃 _____

🙂 _____

853. *Have you ever been in a long-distance relationship? Could you do it or do it again?*

😃 _____

🙂 _____

854. *Have you ever been stalked by anyone? What did you do?*

😃 _____

🙂 _____

855. *Have you ever been in an abusive relationship?*

😃 _____

🙂 _____

856. *Did any of your previous relationships leave you with any serious "scars" or traumas?*

😃 _____

🙂 _____

857. *Is there anyone from your past that you still have strong feelings for?*

☺ ---

☺ ---

858. *Is there anyone from your past who still scares you in any way?*

☺ ---

☺ ---

859. *Do you consider yourself 100% to blame for the end of any of your previous relationships? Why?*

☺ ---

☺ ---

860. *Have you ever talked about marriage with someone previously?*

☺ ---

☺ ---

861. *Have you ever been in a relationship that you wish you never had?*

☺ ---

☺ ---

862. *Does loving someone scare you for any reason?*

☺ ---

☺ ---

863. *Do you still maintain friendships with former partners?*

☺ _____

☺ _____

864. *If your current partner were uncomfortable about any of those friendships, would you end them?*

☺ _____

☺ _____

865. *Do you keep pictures of your past partners?*

☺ _____

☺ _____

866. *Would it bother you if your partner kept photos of past lovers?*

☺ _____

☺ _____

867. *Have you ever dated someone who wanted to wait until marriage to have sex? If yes, is this the reason why your relationship ended?*

☺ _____

☺ _____

868. What do you think is the secret behind couples that have been married for over 30 years and are still happy together?

☺ --

☺ --

869. Of all the people you know, which couple do you think is the happiest? What about their relationship would you like to be able to have?

☺ --

☺ --

870. And which one do you think is the most miserable? What's the main problem with them, in your opinion?

☺ --

☺ --

871. Which couple of your group of friends do you think will inevitably split up?

☺ --

☺ --

872. And why do you think most marriages end up in divorce? What's the number one thing to avoid, in your opinion, to make things work?

☺ --

☺ --

873. If your partner was having serious doubts about themselves or your marriage and wanted to be separated for six months to think things over, would you agree?

☻ _____

☺ _____

874. If yes, would you live as though you were still together, or would you consider yourself free to date and meet new people?

☻ _____

☺ _____

875. In order for you to trust someone, what do you need to see in them?

☻ _____

☺ _____

876. Do you find it overall easy to trust the people you date, or do they have to earn your trust?

☻ _____

☺ _____

877. Has your current partner ever done or said anything that led you to mistrust them?

☻ _____

☺ _____

878. What are the most important things you have learned from your partner?

☻ ....

☺ ....

879. Do your friends generally turn to you for relationship advice?

☻ ....

☺ ....

880. And who do you generally turn to when you need love advice? Or do you prefer to keep your thoughts and feelings to yourself?

☻ ....

☺ ....

881. Have your parents given you any dating advice? Do you trust them on this?

☻ ....

☺ ....

882. What do you think is the best relationship advice you've ever received?

☻ ....

☺ ....

883. *If your partner was really unhappy about you sharing couple's fights/disagreements with your friends or family, would you agree not to do it? Or would you agree to discuss it with them only if you couldn't solve the problem on your own within a few days?*

☺ _____

☺ _____

884. *What mistakes have you seen in other couples that you want to make sure won't happen in your relationship?*

☺ _____

☺ _____

885. *In which ways are you and your partner the same?*

☺ _____

☺ _____

886. *And in which ways do you consider you and your partner to be very different?*

☺ _____

☺ _____

887. *In your opinion, for a relationship to be successful, the two partners need to be very alike or more like opposites?*

☺ _____

☺ _____

888. *Would you live the rest of your life with your partner exactly the way they are now? Or would you like some things to change for you to be able to commit to them?*

☻ _____

☺ _____

889. *Can you recall the exact moment you knew you were falling in love with your current partner?*

☻ _____

☺ _____

890. *Do you think you and your partner have any unresolved issues between you?*

☻ _____

☺ _____

891. *Do you consider that your partner is or acts in a needy way? Only on certain occasions or all the time?*

☻ _____

☺ _____

892. *Do you consider yourself a needy partner?*

☻ _____

☺ _____

893. *What's the number one thing you would like to change about how you are in a relationship?*

☻ _____

☺ _____

894. Do you have a feeling your current partner would like to change any of your qualities or behaviors? Which ones?

☻ ---

☺ ---

895. How would you feel about your partner opening your email or reading your messages? Has this ever happened to you?

☻ ---

☺ ---

896. Have you ever read a partner's private messages or emails? If yes, why?

☻ ---

☺ ---

897. What is your definition of "cheating" on your partner?

☻ ---

☺ ---

898. Do you consider it is cheating if your partner shares sexual thoughts and fantasies online with others?

☻ ---

☺ ---

899. Do you currently have dating apps on your phone?

☻ ---

☺ ---

900. *Would you delete them if your partner asked you to?*

☻ --

☺ --

901. *Have you ever been in a committed relationship and slept with someone else? Why did you do it? Did you feel guilty? Did you tell your partner?*

☻ --

☺ --

902. *Would it hurt you the most if your partner had a one-night stand with a stranger or if you discovered they had real feelings for someone else but no intention to physically cheat on you?*

☻ --

☺ --

903. *Have you ever considered marrying someone because you were afraid that no one else would come along, and you would rather be married than single?*

☻ --

☺ --

904. *Have you ever dated someone you didn't truly love for a long time? If yes, why did you stay with this person?*

☻ --

☺ --

905. Do you think that if a person offends your partner is automatically offending you as well?

☺ _____

☺ _____

906. How much of your time do you offer your partner exclusively? Do you consider it enough?

☺ _____

☺ _____

907. Do you think you and your partner should spend more quality time together?

☺ _____

☺ _____

908. How would you feel if your partner began to spend more time working on their hobbies and talents if that took time away from your relationship?

☺ _____

☺ _____

909. What, if anything, do you feel you need to sacrifice or compromise in your relationship to make it work?

☺ _____

☺ _____

910. *Do you feel you have the personal space you need in your current relationship?*

😃 --

☺ --

911. *Do you consider that the needs of your relationship eclipse your personal needs quite often?*

😃 --

☺ --

912. *Do you think it's healthy for a couple to spend time away from each other occasionally?*

😃 --

☺ --

913. *What are the things that cause the most arguments in your current relationship?*

😃 --

☺ --

914. *Do you think it is healthy for couples to fight (in a non-violent way) from time to time?*

😃 --

☺ --

915. *What do you think about fighting and hurting each other emotionally or physically?*

😃 --

☺ --

916. *How would you feel if your partner raised their voice (shouted) at you?*

☻ _____

☺ _____

917. *Have you ever said anything to your partner that you wish you could take back?*

☻ _____

☺ _____

918. *What do you think is the best way for couples to handle disagreements?*

☻ _____

☺ _____

919. *How do you think your partner manages problems in your relationship? Do they do it the way you would like them to?*

☻ _____

☺ _____

920. *Are you generally the partner who starts the fights or who tries to end them?*

☻ _____

☺ _____

921. How would you like your partner to introduce you to others? (boyfriend/girlfriend, partner, friend, future husband/wife, etc.?)

☻ _____

☺ _____

922. If your partner went to a dance or nightclub without you, how would you feel?

☻ _____

☺ _____

923. Has your current partner ever behaved in such a way around someone that made you feel uncomfortable?

☻ _____

☺ _____

924. Do you consider your partner jealous? Would you like this to change?

☻ _____

☺ _____

925. Are you jealous of any of your current partner's friends or acquaintances?

☻ _____

☺ _____

926. *Do you think someone in your partner's life is in love with them, and they're not aware of it?*

😃 _____

☺ _____

927. *Imagine your partner had to leave each year for work for two months: would you trust them while they are away? Do you think this could strengthen or weaken your relationship?*

😃 _____

☺ _____

928. *Do you feel like your current relationship it is often more work than fun?*

😃 _____

☺ _____

929. *Do you think that this is a sign that something might be wrong, or do you consider that this is how all relationships are?*

😃 _____

☺ _____

930. *If your partner wanted to end things with you, how would they want them to do it?*

😃 _____

☺ _____

931. Is there anything in your past that you need to disclose that might have serious consequences on your current relationship?

☻ _____

☺ _____

932. Is there anything that is keeping you from relaxing and enjoying your current relationship to the fullest?

☻ _____

☺ _____

933. Do you like to post pictures of yourself and your partner on social media? Why or why not?

☻ _____

☺ _____

934. If your partner asked you to stop posting pictures on social media would you agree to do it? Only pictures of the two of you or pictures in general?

☻ _____

☺ _____

935. What would you think if your partner only posted pictures of themselves on social media (no mention at all of your relationship)?

☻ _____

☺ _____

936. *Have you ever acted this way yourself? Why?*

☻ ---

☺ ---

937. *If you died before your wife/husband, would you want them to feel completely free to marry again?*

☻ ---

☺ ---

938. *How long do you think they should wait before dating again?*

☻ ---

☺ ---

939. *In which ways is the opposite sex still an enigma to you?*

☻ ---

☺ ---

Section 20: Children and Parenting

Children can bring so much joy to a couple. But also sleepless nights, headaches, and less time to spend together as a couple. Overall, there is much more to the decision of whether or not to have children than dreaming of the child's gender and the perfect name.

Especially when parents have different views on discipline and child rearing, friction and tension can arise. Piece of advice?

If you haven't already, talk to as many parents as you can before answering the questions in this section. A child is the greatest gift you can receive, but it's also a lot more work than you probably realize right now...

940. *Would you like to have children in the future? Do you think you might change your mind about this?*

😃 _____

🙂 _____

941. *Have you always felt the same way about this topic, or you've only recently started to feel like this?*

😃 _____

🙂 _____

942. *Generally speaking, do you think the decision not to have children is selfish or wise?*

😃 _____

🙂 _____

943. *Do you consider that having children and becoming parents is a right or a desire?*

😃 _____

🙂 _____

944. *Do you feel you need to have children to consider your life "complete"?*

😃 _____

🙂 _____

945. Could you end things with a partner you truly love, but that doesn't share your same vision about having or not having children?

☻ _____

☺ _____

946. Could you have a child with a partner you're not in love with only because you want to become a parent?

☻ _____

☺ _____

947. How do you think you would feel and react if your partner told you that you were expecting?

☻ _____

☺ _____

948. Leaving your partner aside, who would you tell first that you are expecting?

☻ _____

☺ _____

949. Would you like to tell them in a special way? Which one?

☻ _____

☺ _____

950. Would you like to share the good news with more people, or would you prefer to wait a few months and be sure that everything is okay with the pregnancy?

☺ --

☺ --

951. What's the thing that scares you the most about having a child?

☺ --

☺ --

952. Ideally, how many children would you like to have?

☺ --

☺ --

953. How do you think you would react in case of discovering you're expecting twins? Triplets?

☺ --

☺ --

954. Do you strongly wish for a particular gender?

☺ --

☺ --

955. Would you like to have a gender reveal party?

☺ --

☺ --

956. How do you envision it? Who would you like to be in charge of organizing it?

☻ --

☺ --

957. If you wanted a boy (or girl) and you already had two girls (or boys), do you think you would like to keep trying until having a boy (or girl)?

☻ --

☺ --

958. When do you think you should stop trying?

☻ --

☺ --

959. What are the top three qualities you hope your children will have?

☻ --

☺ --

960. If you (or your partner) couldn't get pregnant naturally, what sort of medical treatments would you be willing to consider? For how long?

☻ --

☺ --

961. What are your thoughts on adopting children if you were unable to have a child of your own?

☻ _____

☺ _____

962. Would you prefer a surrogate over adoption?

☻ _____

☺ _____

963. Would you consider adopting even if you could have biological children?

☻ _____

☺ _____

964. If the doctors detected that your unborn child had a severe health problem, would you still have the baby?

☻ _____

☺ _____

965. If you couldn't have children in any way, how would this change your life plan?

☻ _____

☺ _____

966. Would you like to have a baby shower?

☻ _____

☺ _____

967. What's your vision of the perfect baby shower? Who would you like to organize it?

☻ --

☺ --

968. If you are the male partner, would you like to be in the delivery room next to your partner at the moment of your child's birth?

☻ --

☺ --

969. If you are the female partner, would you like to have your partner in the delivery room next to you at the moment of your child's birth, or do you think you would feel more comfortable with someone else?

☻ --

☺ --

970. After the baby is born, how do you think new parents should share the different tasks for taking care of the newborn?

☻ --

☺ --

971. How would you react if your partner didn't want to take care of basic things such as changing diapers and waking up at night to take care of the baby?

☻ --

☺ --

972. Do you think both partners have exactly the same responsibilities in the upbringing of their children?

☻ _____

☺ _____

973. Do you think it is important for a baby to be breastfed for both health reasons and for bonding?

☻ _____

☺ _____

974. If so, how long do you think babies should be breastfed?

☻ _____

☺ _____

975. After your baby is born, would you consider having someone (grandparents or a full-time nanny) move into your home to help you and your partner with the baby?

☻ _____

☺ _____

976. Could you be in a serious relationship with someone who already has children from a previous marriage?

☻ _____

☺ _____

977. If you were a stepparent, what role would you like to play?

☻ _____

☺ _____

978. *If you had children and got divorced, what would you expect from your ex's new partner? What kind of stepparent would you want them to be?*

😃 --

☺ --

979. *If you already have children, what's the thing you found the hardest about raising them?*

😃 --

☺ --

980. *If you already have children with a previous partner, would you agree to have more if your current partner wanted to become a parent?*

😃 --

☺ --

981. *Would you consider staying with a partner you no longer love to offer your children family stability?*

😃 --

☺ --

982. *Would you consider leaving a partner that you love deeply but that it's an unfit parent for your children?*

😃 --

☺ --

983. If you got divorced and had children, what things would you like to do to make this situation as easy as possible for your children?

☻ --

☺ --

984. In which areas do you think parents should sacrifice for their children, and in which areas they should not?

☻ --

☺ --

985. After the birth of your child, how much time would you want to (or could) take off from work?

☻ --

☺ --

986. Do you think one of the parents should stay home with the baby until a certain age?

☻ --

☺ --

987. Which other alternatives do you consider (grandparents, babysitter, nursery, etc.)?

☻ --

☺ --

988. *At what age would you like your child to start going to the nursery?*

☻ _____

☺ _____

989. *If you wanted to become a one-income household after the birth of your child, what lifestyle changes would need to take place?*

☻ _____

☺ _____

990. *Do you have specific preferences about the sort of food you would like your children to eat (vegan, vegetarian, organic, no sugar, etc.)?*

☻ _____

☺ _____

991. *Would you be willing to change your eating habits to match what you think your children should be eating?*

☻ _____

☺ _____

992. *If you had a son, would you want him to be circumcised? Why?*

☻ _____

☺ _____

993. *Do you have any strong preferences for naming your children? Or would you agree to let your partner choose the baby's name?*

😃 ....

🙂 ....

994. *Would you consider moving to an area that has a really good school system for your children?*

😃 ....

🙂 ....

995. *Would you consider moving to another area or city to have your family close while raising your child?*

😃 ....

🙂 ....

996. *How do you think you would react if your or your partner's parents didn't want to help you take care of the baby?*

😃 ....

🙂 ....

997. *And how would you react if they were "too present"?*

😃 ....

🙂 ....

998. Would you want your children to be home-schooled? Why or why not?

☺ _____

☺ _____

999. Have you already read any books on parenting?

☺ _____

☺ _____

1000. Do you think it is a good idea to read "expert" books, or it's better just follow your instinct when it comes to parenting?

☺ _____

☺ _____

1001. What sort of limitations do you think you would want to place on your children regarding television, magazines, social media, mobile phones, video games, etc.?

☺ _____

☺ _____

1002. Which, if any, household chores would you expect your children to do? Starting at what age?

☺ _____

☺ _____

1003. Have you thought about how you would want to discipline your children during childhood and teen years?

1004. How do you think you will talk to your children about "hard topics" (drugs, sex, etc.)?

1005. If you were offered a great job opportunity that meant spending most of your time away from your family, would you accept it?

1006. Do you think you would give up your job to spend more time with your children?

1007. Would you regularly give financial support to your adult children? Why or why not?

1008. Do you think it is natural for parents to love their offspring more than their partner?

☻ _____

☺ _____

1009. Would you like to be a young parent or to have children later in life? Why?

☻ _____

☺ _____

1010. At what age do you think you would be too old to have children to really enjoy them?

☻ _____

☺ _____

1011. In your opinion, what kind of relationship should a couple have, and what kind of financial stability should they count on before trying to have children?

☻ _____

☺ _____

1012. Ideally, what are the minimum number of years you think you would need to build a solid relationship before trying for a baby?

☻ _____

☺ _____

1013. What are the reasons why a couple should have children? What are the reasons why they should not?

☻ --

☺ --

1014. How do you think your relationship would change as a result of having a baby?

☻ --

☺ --

1015. If you knew with 100% certainty that having children would decrease your marital satisfaction by 40%, would you still want children?

☻ --

☺ --

1016. What would you like to do to keep the passion alive in your relationship after becoming parents?

☻ --

☺ --

1017. How were you shown affection as a child? Do you think you will show your children affection the same way or differently?

☻ --

☺ --

1018. Do you plan on raising your children in a similar way to how you were raised, very differently, or something in between?

😃 _____

🙂 _____

1019. Is there anything that your parents did that you would never ever do when bringing up your children?

😃 _____

🙂 _____

1020. What kind of school would you like your child to go to?

😃 _____

🙂 _____

1021. If your child should be the victim of bullying at school, what do you think you would do?

😃 _____

🙂 _____

1022. Do you wish them to go to a particular college or study a specific career?

😃 _____

🙂 _____

1023. *Do you think that your advice to your child will be to follow their passions and do what they like in life or to choose a career that will allow them to have financial stability?*

☻ --

☺ --

1024. *How do you feel about posting pictures of your children on social media?*

☻ --

☺ --

Section 21: Wedding and Honeymoon

The wedding and honeymoon are supposed to be among the happiest events in a couple's lives, yet they often end up being the first major disappointments.

Friends, family, money, religion, and time all come into play, creating a potentially explosive combination. But again, with knowledge, communication, and mutual understanding, you and your partner can create wonderful memories that will last a lifetime.

1025. *If your partner had a bachelor or bachelorette party, is there anything they might do that you would find inappropriate?*

☻ --

☺ --

1026.   Would you agree to not allow anything to happen at your bachelor or bachelorette party that your partner deems inappropriate?

☻ ....

☺ ....

1027.   If you want a bachelor or bachelorette party, who would you like to attend it?

☻ ....

☺ ....

1028.   Would you consider an offbeat wedding (underwater, on a roller coaster, etc.)?

☻ ....

☺ ....

1029.   Would you consider eloping? Why or why not?

☻ ....

☺ ....

1030.   Would you consider hiring a wedding planner for your wedding?

☻ ....

☺ ....

1031.   Where would you like to get married?

☻ ....

☺ ....

1032. How many of your friends and family would you like to invite to your wedding?

☻ ....

☺ ....

1033. What's the maximum number of people you would like to have at your wedding?

☻ ....

☺ ....

1034. Would you agree to have more than 300 people at your wedding if that was your partner's wish?

☻ ....

☺ ....

1035. Would you agree to have just a few people at your wedding if that was your partner's wish?

☻ ....

☺ ....

1036. What's your vision of the perfect wedding?

☻ ....

☺ ....

1037. What's your vision of the perfect wedding dress for the bride?

☻ ....

☺ ....

1038. *How much do you think is acceptable to pay for a wedding dress?*

☻ --

☺ --

1039. *1006 Would you like you and your partner to have matching wedding rings?*

☻ --

☺ --

1040. *What's your vision of the perfect engagement ring?*

☻ --

☺ --

1041. *How much do you think it's acceptable to pay for an engagement ring?*

☻ --

☺ --

1042. *Who would you tell first that you and your partner are engaged?*

☻ --

☺ --

1043. Would you like to let this person know it in a particular way?

☻ ....

☺ ....

1044. Is there anyone special you would like to officiate at your wedding?

☻ ....

☺ ....

1045. What's your vision of the perfect wedding proposal?

☻ ....

☺ ....

1046. If someone helped you pay for your wedding (or part of it), do you think they should have some sort of control over the ceremony plans?

☻ ....

☺ ....

1047. Would you allow your parents or your partner's parents to decide things or invite people to your wedding?

☻ ....

☺ ....

1048. How long do you think it's necessary to plan a wedding?

☻ --

☺ --

1049. If you already have children, in which way would you like them to participate in your wedding?

☻ --

☺ --

1050. Would you feel awkward if your partner invited former partners or lovers to the wedding?

☻ --

☺ --

1051. Is there any ex-partner or lover of yours you would like to invite to your wedding?

☻ --

☺ --

1052. Is there any friends o relatives of your partner that you wouldn't want to attend your wedding? Why? Would you accept them to attend if that was important for your partner?

☻ --

☺ --

1053. *Is there any friends o relatives of yours that you wouldn't want to attend your wedding? Why?*

☻ ....

☺ ....

1054. *Have you been married before? If yes, what would you do in a different way this second time regarding the wedding ceremony?*

☻ ....

☺ ....

1055. *Do you think a woman should take a man's last name?*

☻ ....

☺ ....

1056. *Would you consider hyphenated last names for both partners?*

☻ ....

☺ ....

1057. *How much time off do you think you could take for your honeymoon?*

☻ ....

☺ ....

1058. *Would you accept spending your honeymoon in a place you have no interest in visiting if that was your partner's dream destination?*

☺ _____

☺ _____

1059. *What's your honeymoon dream destination?*

☺ _____

☺ _____

1060. *How much do you consider acceptable spending for a honeymoon?*

☺ _____

☺ _____

1061. *Would you consider going on your honeymoon with best friends or close relatives too?*

☺ _____

☺ _____

Section 22: Let's Talk about Sex

I'm sure many of you skipped the other sections and came straight to this one: this is where the fun is, right? Some of you, however, may wish these questions weren't here at all, and may feel embarrassed at the idea of talking about this topic. However, discussing sex openly and respectfully is a great way to build a deeper connection between you and your significant other and avoid problems that could cause serious difficulties in your relationship.

At the same time, if you haven't had sex yet and want to wait, it's perfectly fine to skip this section for now, or start with just a few questions to get to know your partner a little better. After all, when it comes to sex, neither of you should feel pressured to do anything you don't want to!

1062. *Do you think talking about sex can help make it a better experience for you and your partner?*

☻ _____

☺ _____

1063. *What makes a person sexy for you?*

☻ _____

☺ _____

1064. *What body parts turn you on the most?*

☻ _____

☺ _____

1065. *And which part of your partner's body do you find more attractive?*

☻ _____

☺ _____

1066. *Is there a particular scent that you find particularly sexy?*

☻ _____

☺ _____

1067.   *What kind of clothing do you find sexy?*

😃 _____

🙂 _____

1068.   *And what kind of clothing has the opposite effect on you and turns you off?*

😃 _____

🙂 _____

1069.   *What sort of lingerie/underwear do you find sexy?*

😃 _____

🙂 _____

1070.   *Do you tend to feel more attracted by people who are explicitly sexy or more discreet?*

😃 _____

🙂 _____

1071.   *Are there any particular songs that make you think of having sex/making love?*

😃 _____

🙂 _____

1072.   *Is there anything that you know of that works as an aphrodisiac for you?*

😃 _____

🙂 _____

1073.   *Do you consider yourself sexy? Why or why not?*

☻ --

☺ --

1074.   *What are the three most sensitive areas of your body?*

☻ --

☺ --

1075.   *And what parts of your own body do you consider sexier?*

☻ --

☺ --

1076.   *Some people think that "size matters" (breast, penis, etc.): what are your thoughts and/or experiences about it?*

☻ --

☺ --

1077.   *Have you had sex before?*

☻ --

☺ --

1078.   *If not, why?*

☻ --

☺ --

1079. *If you plan to abstain from sex until marriage, what sort of physical contact do you consider acceptable (kissing, petting, etc.)?*

😀 _____

🙂 _____

1080. *Do you think it is important for a couple to have sex the first night they are married? If it has been a long and tiring day, would that make any difference?*

😀 _____

🙂 _____

1081. *Did your parents ever discuss their views on sex with you?*

😀 _____

🙂 _____

1082. *How many sexual partners have you had?*

😀 _____

🙂 _____

1083. *Was your first time a good or a bad experience?*

😀 _____

🙂 _____

1084. *How old were you?*

😀 _____

🙂 _____

1085. *What turns you on the most sexually?*

☻ --

☺ --

1086. *And what turns you off?*

☻ --

☺ --

1087. *Have you had one-night stands?*

☻ --

☺ --

1088. *According to you, sex and love go hand in hand, or are they two completely different things?*

☻ --

☺ --

1089. *Do you need to like somebody very much to go to bed with them, or that's not necessary at all?*

☻ --

☺ --

1090. *Have you had sex mostly with people you truly liked (or loved) or with people who were "available" at that moment?*

☻ --

☺ --

1091. *In your sex life, have you had more sex or made more love?*

☻ --

☺ --

1092. *Have you ever felt sexually used?*

☻ --

☺ --

1093. *How has your sexuality changed over the years?*

☻ --

☺ --

1094. *Do you think a person's sexual past matters if you really love them?*

☻ --

☺ --

1095. *Do you feel confident about sex, or do you consider you still have much to learn?*

☻ --

☺ --

1096. *Do you believe that when it comes to sex if it feels good that it must be okay to do?*

☻ --

☺ --

1097. *Have you ever thought you could be sexually addicted?*

☻ ....

☺ ....

1098. *Is it difficult for you to ask your partner to stimulate you in a certain way?*

☻ ....

☺ ....

1099. *Do you believe that when a couple has sex for the first time, some sort of commitment occurs?*

☻ ....

☺ ....

1100. *Do you prefer to have sex in the morning or at night?*

☻ ....

☺ ....

1101. *Do you generally prefer making love in the dark, with candlelight, or with the lights on?*

☻ ....

☺ ....

1102. *Do you feel shy/embarrassed being naked in front of your partner?*

☻ ....

☺ ....

1103.   *Do you have a favorite foreplay activity to turn you on?*

☻ _____

☺ _____

1104.   *How does foreplay enhance your sexual experience?*

☻ _____

☺ _____

1105.   *What is your favorite sex position?*

☻ _____

☺ _____

1106.   *And the one you enjoy the least?*

☻ _____

☺ _____

1107.   *What sexual act have you never done before but would like to try?*

☻ _____

☺ _____

1108.   *Do you like to be visually stimulated while making love?*

☻ _____

☺ _____

1109. Do you think it would be fun to use sex toys with your partner?

☺ ....

☻ ....

1110. Do you think it would be fun to read the Kamasutra with your partner?

☺ ....

☻ ....

1111. Do you generally prefer sex to be "hard" or "gentle"?

☺ ....

☻ ....

1112. Is there a particular place where you would like to have sex?

☺ ....

☻ ....

1113. What's the strangest place you've ever had sex at?

☺ ....

☻ ....

1114. Is there anything you would never do in bed, even if your partner asked you to?

☺ ....

☻ ....

1115.   Is there anything sexual you find wrong or offensive?

☻ --

☺ --

1116.   For the female partner: are there certain times of the month that your breasts are sensitive and/or that you don't like them to be touched?

☻ --

☺ --

1117.   What does your current partner do that gives you the most pleasure?

☻ --

☺ --

1118.   Given your current sex drive, how many times a day would you like to make love with your partner?

☻ --

☺ --

1119.   On a scale of 1-10, how strong do you think your sex drive is?

☻ --

☺ --

1120.   *How would you define satisfying sex?*

☻ --

☺ --

1121.   *Would you want your partner to let you know if you haven't sexually satisfied them?*

☻ --

☺ --

1122.   *How would you like them to tell you?*

☻ --

☺ --

1123.   *In a relationship, do you think that one should mostly focus on pleasing themselves during sex or pleasing their partner? Why?*

☻ --

☺ --

1124.   *Do you like to cuddle after sex? Do you think you and your current partner are on the same page on this?*

☻ --

☺ --

1125.   *Are there times when you just want a "quickie"? When are those?*

☻ --

☺ --

1126. Do you prefer your partner to make the first move, or you rather do it yourself?

☻ _____

☺ _____

1127. Do you feel masturbation is okay? Do you practice it?

☻ _____

☺ _____

1128. What about when it is accompanied by sexual thoughts of someone besides your partner?

☻ _____

☺ _____

1129. Would you do a threesome? Have you before?

☻ _____

☺ _____

1130. Would you role-play while having sex?

☻ _____

☺ _____

1131. Would you like to videotape yourself and your partner while making love?

☻ _____

☺ _____

1132.   Would you like to have sex outdoors?

☻ --

☺ --

1133.   Do you have any sexual fetishes?

☻ --

☺ --

1134.   Would you like to take showers with your partner on a regular basis, only every once in a while, or do you prefer to take them alone?

☻ --

☺ --

1135.   Do you think you and your partner could or should have sex even though you are currently mad at each other?

☻ --

☺ --

1136.   Do you think the daily number of times you make love with your partner should increase when you go on vacation?

☻ --

☺ --

1137.   Would you feel comfortable having sex at your friend's house or your parent's house?

☺ --

☺ --

1138.   Do you think it is wise to go to counseling for sexual problems? If not, how would you want to try to work out problems of this kind?

☺ --

☺ --

1139.   When making love with your partner, do you often feel that your partner is doing it just to make you happy?

☺ --

☺ --

1140.   Do you think it is possible for a couple to have sex too often? What problems could it cause?

☺ --

☺ --

1141.   Do you think it is appropriate to use sex as a "negotiating" tool in a couple? Is it ever healthy for a couple to withhold sex from their partner?

☺ --

☺ --

1142. Do you think two people that love each other deeply but don't have a satisfactory sex life can work as a couple?

1143. Do you think that two people that have a great sex life but fight about everything else can work as a couple?

1144. How do you feel when your partner tells you they're not in the mood for sex?

1145. Do you think sex is overrated?

1146. Do you think that you might have a difficult time enjoying sex because of previous sexual experiences or because of what you were taught about sex while growing up?

1147. Do you talk with someone about your sex life? Would you stop doing it if your partner asked you to?

☻ ---

☺ ---

1148. And what sort of sexual things do you discuss with your friends in general?

☻ ---

☺ ---

1149. According to your experience, do condoms significantly reduce the enjoyment of sex? Do they help prevent premature ejaculation?

☻ ---

☺ ---

1150. What method of birth control do you prefer? Why?

☻ ---

☺ ---

1151. Would you consider getting your tubes tied or having a vasectomy?

☻ ---

☺ ---

1152. *Are there any forms of birth control you will not use?*

🙂 ....

🙂 ....

1153. *Would you get tested for sexually transmitted diseases if your partner asked you to?*

🙂 ....

🙂 ....

1154. *How do you think sex changes as a couple grows older together?*

🙂 ....

🙂 ....

1155. *How do you think having children changes the sexual life of a couple?*

🙂 ....

🙂 ....

1156. *Do you have any concerns about having sex during pregnancy?*

🙂 ....

🙂 ....

1157. *What do you think a couple should do to keep the "flame" alive?*

🙂 ....

🙂 ....

1158. *How do you think your sex life with your partner could become even better?*

☻ --

☺ --

Conclusions

Thank you so much for reading and using this book: I sincerely hope you and your partner have had a great time together and that you will be able to build a strong and healthy relationship.

If these questions have helped you to get to know your other half better, please don't forget to leave your honest opinion about this book on the corresponding Amazon page: QR book page

I wish you both a lifetime of happiness!